Issue 2 June 1998

Edited by Dr. Valerie Steele

Fashion Theory

The Journal of Dress, Body & Culture

BERG

Fashion Theory: The Journal of Dress, Body & Culture

Editor
Dr. Valerie Steele
The Museum at the Fashion Institute of Technology, E201
Seventh Avenue at 27th Street
New York, NY 10001-5992
USA
Fax: +1 212 924 3958
e-mail: steelemajor@earthlink.net

Aims and Scope

The importance of studying the body as a site for the deployment of discourses is well-established in a number of disciplines. By contrast, the study of fashion has, until recently, suffered from a lack of critical analysis. Increasingly, however, scholars have recognized the cultural significance of self-fashioning, including not only clothing but also such body alterations as tattooing and piercing. *Fashion Theory* takes as its starting point a definition of 'fashion' as the cultural construction of the embodied identity. It aims to provide an interdisciplinary forum for the rigorous analysis of cultural phenomena ranging from footbinding to fashion advertising.

Anyone wishing to submit an article, interview, or a book, film or exhibition review for possible publication in this journal should contact Valerie Steele (at the address listed below) or the Editorial Department at Berg (150 Cowley Road, Oxford, OX4 1JJ, UK; e-mail: enquiry@berg.demon.co.uk).

Notes for Contributors can be found at the back of the journal.

© 1998 Berg. All rights reserved. No part of this publication may be reproduced or utilized in any form or by any means, electronic or mechanical, including photocopying and recording, or by any information storage or retrieval system, without permission in writing from the Publisher.

ISSN: 1362-704X

Editorial Board

Christopher Breward
Royal College of Art, UK

Patrizia Calefato
University of Bari, Italy

Joanne B. Eicher
University of Minnesota, USA

Caroline Evans
Central Saint Martins College of Art and Design, UK

Anne Hollander
New York Institute for the Humanities, USA

Susan Kaiser
University of California at Davis, USA

Dorothy Ko
Rutgers University, USA

Edward Maeder
Bata Shoe Museum, Canada

Richard Martin
The Metropolitan Museum of Art, USA

Anne McClintock
Columbia University, USA

Philippe Perrot
École des Hautes Études, France

Aileen Ribeiro
Courtauld Institute of Art, UK

Jane Schneider
City University of New York, USA

Lou Taylor
University of Brighton, UK

Efrat Tseëlon
Leeds Metropolitan University, UK

Elizabeth Wilson
University of North London, UK

Ordering Information Four issues per volume. One volume per annum. 1998: Volume 2

By mail: Berg Publishers, 150 Cowley Road, Oxford, OX4 1JJ, UK.

By fax: +44 (0) 1865 791165

By telephone: +44 (0) 1865 245104

By e-mail: enquiry@berg.demon.co.uk

Inquiries

Editorial: Kathryn Earle, Managing Editor, e-mail: kearle@berg1.demon.co.uk

Production: Sara Everett, e-mail: severett@berg.demon.co.uk

Advertising + subscriptions: Paul Millicheap, e-mail: pmillicheap@berg.demon.co.uk

Subscription Rates:

Institutional base list subscription price: £86.00, US$120.00.

Individuals' subscription price: £35.00, US$48.00.

Reprints of Individual Articles

Copies of individual articles may be obtained from the Publishers at the appropriate fees. Write to: Berg, 150 Cowley Road, Oxford, OX4 1JJ, UK.

Printed in the United Kingdom.
JUNE 1998

Page 111

Page 129

Page 165

Contents

Editor
Dr. Valerie Steele
The Museum at the Fashion Institute of Technology, E201
Seventh Avenue at 27th Street
New York, NY 10001-5992
USA

Fax +1 212 924 3958
e-mail: steelemajor@earthlink.net

BERG

Dedication

All the staff at Berg would like to dedicate this issue of *Fashion Theory* to:

Peter D. Cowell
(1937–1998).

Through his faith, his grace and his generosity of spirit, this journal, and so much more, exists.

With love and gratitude.

BERG

Fashion Theory, Volume 2, Issue 2, pp.109–110
Reprints available directly from the Publishers.
Photocopying permitted by licence only.

© Roxanne Lowit

Letter from the Editor

A friend in Paris just sent me a newspaper clipping from the *International Herald Tribune* (1/27/98). In her article "Prosthetic as Beauty Aesthetic" fashion journalist Suzy Menkes reports that "For his fashion show on Saturday, the maverick Belgian designer Walter Van Beirendonck came up with prosthetic attachments to the faces of male and female models, changing the shapes of noses, chins and cheeks, or giving them more dramatic lumps and bumps." The *Tribune* printed photographs of the fashion models, showing cosmetic sculpting that resembles scarification. At a time when piercing and tattooing have become commonplace, such facial transformations may become the latest club cult.

Van Beirendonck says that he was inspired by the French conceptual artist Orlan, who has repeatedly undergone cosmetic surgery to transform herself into a living art work. Ever on the cutting edge, this issue of *Fashion Theory* features an article on Orlan by Kate Ince, which analyzes the surgical project within the context of a discussion of the skin. By "skin," however, she means not only the epidermis itself, but also the way dress functions as a kind of "second skin" or bodily envelope. Ince is currently writing a book on Orlan which will explore these ideas further, and I am delighted that the readers of *Fashion Theory* will get a preview of her work.

The thin and abject models in fashion photography are often described as looking like "skin and bones." As Katharine Wallerstein points out,

"This aesthetic has been attacked as an inducement to anorexia [or] as heroin chic." Advertising posters of Kate Moss, for example, have been defaced by slogans saying "FEED ME!" In her article, "Thinness and Other Refusals in Contemporary Fashion Advertisements," Wallerstein suggests a more complicated reading of these ads.

Although many people today are convinced that fashion "causes" anorexia in young women by promoting images of whippet-thin models, the reality is more complex. Does country-and-western music *cause* adultery and alcoholism? As obesity becomes ever commoner in the industrialized world (and particularly in the United States), such complaints about fashion's pernicious influences are likely to escalate. It is important, therefore, to question this kind of received wisdom.

Does fashion really promote the "Beauty Myth?" Does it injure young people's self-esteem, cause anorexia, or lead them to abuse drugs? And if so—*how*? It is not enough to imply a Monkey See, Monkey Do cause-and-effect. In the days before he had something more concrete to worry about, even Bill Clinton attacked so-called "heroin chic." Has something in the *Zeitgeist* profoundly changed, now that Calvin Klein's advertisements feature smiling, healthy-looking models? And what about the growing popularity of plastic surgery? Often attacked as grotesquely "unnatural," plastic surgery is not necessarily a form of self-hatred and self-mutilation. This issue of *Fashion Theory* indirectly explores several of the most influential critiques of fashion.

Sincerely yours,

Valerie Steele

Fashion Theory, Volume 2, Issue 2, pp.111–128
Reprints available directly from the Publishers.
Photocopying permitted by licence only.

Operations of Redress: Orlan, the Body and Its Limits

Kate Ince

Kate Ince is Lecturer in French Studies at the University of Birmingham, UK. Her teaching and research interests are in modern French fiction, cinema and the visual arts, and in critical, literary and feminist theory. She has co-edited *French Erotic Fiction: Women's Desiring Writing 1880–1990* (Berg, 1996), and written articles on Marguerite Duras, Luce Irigaray, and issues in literary theory. She is currently co-editing the Longman Critical Reader on Samuel Beckett, and writing a book-length study of Orlan for Berg, to appear in 2000.

The Story of Orlan

Orlan is a French performance artist whose performances, for the last seven years, have consisted of cosmetic surgery. She has taken the term "operating theatre" literally, and is embarked on a project, entitled "The Reincarnation of Saint Orlan," that consists of performing—remaining conscious throughout, photographing, filming and broadcasting—a series of operations that are totally remodeling her face and body, and thus her identity.

"The Reincarnation of Saint Orlan" began in 1990 and is now nearing completion. Saint Orlan is a persona "Orlan" (not her real name) adopted in 1971, a persona she performed by exhibiting and having herself photographed draped in billowing robes made of fabrics such as black vinyl and white leatherette. Uppermost in her intentions in creating these elaborate sculpted costumes was play with religious iconography: the figures of the Virgin Mary and of the ecstatic Saint Theresa of Bernini's famous statue were the basis of these tableaux and of a number of subsequent performances.[1] According to the critic Barbara Rose, the incarnation as Saint Orlan "focused on the hypocrisy of the way society has traditionally split the female image into madonna and whore" (Rose 1993: 84). This strong feminist slant can be detected in the exposure of one breast in the photographs of these tableaux, in the way it apes depictions of the nursing Virgin Mary whilst also being half-way to a page 3 pin-up.

The 1990 (and ongoing) *re*incarnation of Saint Orlan both marks a continuation of Orlan's earlier concerns and a break with them.

Figure 1
"White virgin, objectively seen," 1973. Black and white photograph mounted on wood, 100cm × 100cm. (Photo SIPA Press, Paris).

Religious imagery abounds in the staging of Orlan's operations, and it is difficult to ignore the parallel between religious martyrdom and the suffering (although Orlan argues it otherwise) inflicted by surgery undergone for aesthetic reasons. Orlan's project of bodily reincarnation via cosmetic surgery has been carefully planned from the beginning. There was, however, a degree of chance at the outset of the work: "Due to speak at a symposium in New York, she felt ill, needed emergency surgery and decided to take a video crew along. The resulting tape was immediately rushed across town and shown in her place at the symposium" (McClellan 1994: 40). Further information suggests a more macabre side to this 1978 inspiration to incorporate surgery into her work: "The idea of turning surgical interventions into performance art occurred to her when she was operated on for an extra-uterine pregnancy under a local anaesthetic" (Rose 1993: 84)—more macabre because the life of a fetus was at stake, even if its chances of survival were minimal, but also because the local anesthetic would have allowed Orlan to play the role of detached observer as well as patient during the operation. Orlan's split or double role as object of surgery but also viewer of the operations she chooses to undergo is, as may already be obvious, an essential aspect of her work.

The first official installment of Orlan's self-reinvention took place on 30 May 1990. It was the beginning of a planned sequence of seven operations, each of which was to focus on a specific feature of Orlan's face. There was and is no *one* model for Orlan's self-remodeling; each feature is surgically resculpted to match a specific feature of a different great icon in the history of Western art: the nose of a famous unattributed School of Fontainebleau sculpture of Diana, the mouth of Boucher's

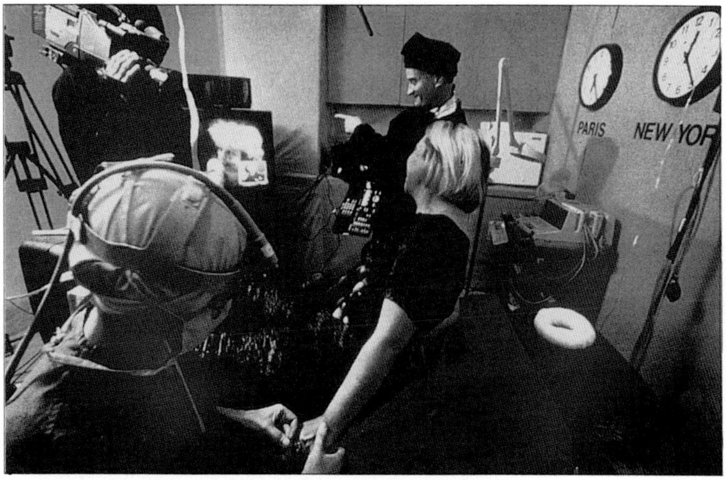

Figure 2
"Atmosphere in the operating theatre before the reading of Eugénie Lemoine-Luccioni for the 7th surgical operation/ performance in New York, 1993." Cibachrome in vacuum diasec, 165cm × 100cm. (Photo SIPA Press, Paris).

Europa, the forehead of Leonardo's *Mona Lisa*, the chin of Botticelli's *Venus* and the eyes of Gérome's *Psyche* (these icons were chosen not for their beauty but for their mythological or historical significance—for example the androgyny of the *Mona Lisa*). Either pastiche or parody of the fetishistic fragmentation of the female body by male artists is clearly intended. She also uses the fragmented character of the image she is composing to effect in her operations/performances, where the aesthetic genre of the detail is advertised by the display of reproductions of just the faces of her various icons. An accentuation of this effect is created by the highlighting, on each reproduction, of the feature to be copied.

The Future Female?

Perhaps the most immediately arresting aspect of Orlan's self-remodeling is the use it makes of computer technology. The new face she is on the way to acquiring was put together digitally, on a computer screen, as a mixture of her own features and the iconic ones she is three-dimensionally reconstructing. Experimentation with new technology—holograms and lasers—already formed part of Orlan's work in the 1980s. Her November 1993 operation, *Omnipresence*, in which implants were inserted above her eyebrows in imitation of the Mona Lisa's forehead, was transmitted live from New York to 14 galleries around the world. (This is a change that Jim McClellan (1994: 38) likens to a diabolic sprouting of horns.) During the five-hour operation the viewers in those galleries could ask the fully conscious Orlan questions by fax.

Orlan herself does see her surgical reincarnation as intimately bound up with the ever more sophisticated technology of the information superhighway. She says: "The whole core of this work is to do with the status of the human body in our present society and in the future. We're changing, mutating. We'll change even more with genetic manipulation. *The body is obsolete*" (quoted in McClellan 1994: 40–2).

The journalist who did the *Observer* piece on (and interview with) Orlan that that quotation comes from is Jim McClellan, author of the paper's weekly *Cyberspace* column. In the article, seemingly slightly taken aback by Orlan's remarkable pronouncement about the obsolescence of the body, he explains:

> This echoes a strain in post-modern theory and science fiction which suggests that rampant technological development is forcing a kind of evolution beyond the body, into a new post-humanity. Our leftover monkey bodies were pretty good when it came to hunting and gathering [. . .] but now that we're thinking about heading off to outer space, now that we spend more and more

> time pushing information around in cyberspace, they're a primitive hangover, an embarrassing encumbrance. It's time for a redesign (1994: 42).

The interest Orlan's project bears for cybertheorists and cyberartists can most easily be illustrated by the comparison Orlan herself makes between her work and that of Stelarc, the Australian male artist who argues that the recent huge increase in social practices such as body-building and cosmetic surgery "are the signs of a desperate, obsolete body beginning to feel it's at the end stage of its evolutionary development" (McClellan 1994: 42). McClellan dubs Stelarc and Orlan the post-human Adam and Eve. He does detect differences between the two artists, in so far as (as he puts it) Stelarc believes that DNA wants to go to space and he is just helping it on its way, whereas Orlan talks about struggling with her DNA, seemingly more aware of the body's resistance to its imminent digitalization. But Orlan does seem to see her surgical change of identity as a kind of race with technology, and does express an undeniable desire for the future. This comes out most strikingly when she says:

> If I wanted to create a nose like a rhinoceros, to have huge waves and bends in it, I wouldn't be able to find a surgeon prepared to do it, or a prosthetic laboratory where they would produce the necessary parts. Actually, surgeons have said to me that what I'm requesting may only be possible in 50 years' time (McClellan 1994: 40).

Her desire for self-transformation outstrips current technological capacity. This, I think, is a strong point in favor of the argument that Orlan, whatever else she is, is also a genuine experimental artist, and not just an exploiter of the hyped-up rhetoric of all things cyber.

One current of cybertheory claims that so-called "advanced" Western cultures are witnessing a gradual eclipsing of the body. Humanity is entering a new phase of its history in which any "component" of the body can be altered or fabricated. Oxygen-permeable synthetic skin will obviate the need for lungs; in fact, bodies without organs altogether will have more space for lots of lovely technology. (Who knows, the replicants—the name given to this kind of post-human being in Ridley Scott's 1982 film *Bladerunner*—might even turn out to be capable of love.)

However, to acknowledge that there is a tendency to deny the body, or at least a claim that it can be left behind, is not the same thing as admitting to its desuetude. Some of Orlan's critics link her work to the technologization of the body, to the increasing dominance in Western societies of technologies of the self, and this side of cyberargument seems very relevant to Orlan's project. But if one is persuaded by the validity of ideas that condone, recommend or predict the obsolescence of the body, why bother to redesign it at all?

Orlan does not *have* a body, she *is* one. And however great the modifications effected in the course of her reincarnation, she will still be one. The permanency of the self-transformation she is carrying out is perhaps the most disturbing aspect of her project; although she intends, plans and choreographs her surgical performances, the different body she is left with after each operation is not something she can totally control. Although it is at the core of her work, the art object *par excellence*, Orlan's body in some sense also escapes the very artistic process it makes possible. At one point in the McClellan interview she appears to recognize this, saying "The biggest danger I face as an artist is that people will become so seduced by my body, by the body in the process of performance, that they will cease to perceive me as an artist" (McClellan 1994: 42). If the audience is focusing on her body, they aren't focusing on her art; the two can never entirely overlap. A definition of the body becomes possible in which it "is," rather than any stable, grounded entity, a remainder or residue that can never be fully worked into the artistic process. Orlan's work brings out—makes visible—the paradox inherent in the very expression "body art."[2]

Operations of Redress

In the dress and fashion industries the object is most often the female body. Dress is nothing without a body on which to hang its cut, its folds and its drapes. Other possible uses of the English "dress" (derived from the Old French *dresser* meaning "to prepare" and/or *drecier* meaning "to arrange"), such as dressing a window and dressing a precious stone or jewelry, remind us of the necessity of having an object to work on. Body and dress function as an opposition that brings more familiar sets of binary oppositions to mind—depth/surface, nature/culture foremost among them. If the body, at least prior to the advent of recent feminist theory, which has stressed its discursivity and thus its constructedness, is often thought of as a (natural) object, dress is, by contrast, studied for its signifying properties, and if conceived of as a system, for its semiotics. Dress is social and cultural, even superficial: in the words of the German philosopher and sociologist Georg Simmel, it is the *superfluity* of adornment that "allows the mere *having* of the person to become a visible quality of its *being*" (Simmel 1985). The body, on the other hand, contains reaches of depth, privacy and eroticism with which dress cannot compete. Although it might appear possible to see the body as a layered structure, in which skin covers muscles that themselves enclose a patterned arteriovenous network, it is almost always viewed as a solid, sealed, unflayable entity.

However, a completely different relationship of the body to dress can be imagined—indeed, has been imagined, and is being worn. In this section I would like to discuss the context that has brought this different relationship about, why the transformation is so important, and how the use of dress and of the body in Orlan's work, both pre-surgical and surgical, offers prime illustrations of developments in dress and fashion in the 1980s and 1990s.

Piercing, tattooing, scarring (or "scarification") and cosmetic surgery make up a group of practices that all involve the skin, and that have all risen to prominence in the West in the 1990s. They are a subset of a larger group of activities that include transsexualism, bodybuilding and rarer practices such as waist-training (corsetry has also recently begun to figure prominently in the work of major fashion designers such as Vivienne Westwood) for which the term "body modification" has been coined. Many of these practices have emerged in contemporary Western urban culture from very specific removes, either social, historical or geographical. For example, tattooing was once the preserve of sailors, gypsies and criminals, whilst piercing has an intriguing past in aristocratic and royal circles, whence it somehow found an echo in the punk practice of sticking safety-pins through the flesh, as well as through clothing. Chinese footbinding and the rainforest Native Americans who wear plates in their lips are examples of body-modification practices in societies once remote from Western influence. Those body-modification practices that involve the skin usually imply permanent alteration of the body's appearance, although they are not all necessarily carried out with the intention of drawing blood or inflicting pain. Whereas tattooing appears to be a highly individualistic activity, doubtless because of the designing of motifs it involves, contemporary Western scarification seems to be based to a large degree around the shared pleasure of sessions devoted to blood-letting. The rings and studs of piercing may be used in sexual play—a good indication of the proximity of some of these practices to the culture of sadomasochism.[3]

In all these body modification activities, it is the skin that is being worked on. The skin has become a site of investigation, and an element in the dress of the people whose bodies have been scarred, pierced or tattooed. In the same way in which, as a viewer, it is difficult to ignore a scar or other disfigurement on the visible body of a person passed in the street, the eye is drawn to the scarification patterns, or the point at which the pierce has been inserted, on someone whose practice of body modification is evident. The identificatory sensibility that comes into play when viewing skin altered by an activity such as piercing or scarring, I am suggesting, makes its wearer even more noticeable than someone sporting the latest fashion (or the latest technology) in design or in fabrics. At the same time, the advertisement of the skin that accompanies certain kinds of body modification, and the growing currency of skin alteration as a cultural practice amongst Western urban populations, means that it is becoming impossible not to admit it to "the fashion system."

The particular point I want to make about this is that accepting the skin as an element of "dress code" does not just represent an enlargement of what we conventionally understand by "dress." It does represent such an enlargement; but it also implies at least two other important changes. The first of these is a change in the status of skin. This takes place through the destabilization of the binary oppositions that the semiotics of dress leaves in place. The skin is the border or limit between the "body inner" and the "body outer" (the visible body). It is the container on which the distinction of inside and outside depends. The skin, it begins to become apparent, is central to the underpinning of a metaphysical conception of the body. Whereas the skin has traditionally been conceived of as a "natural" layer or membrane, it becomes, when body modification practices are admitted as forms of dress, as "cultural" as jeans or polyester.

The second change, related to but perhaps outstripping the first, is a challenge to the traditional metaphysical definition of the body, in which the skin acts as its container or its "envelope" (to borrow a figure from Luce Irigaray's (1984) reading of phallogocentric philosophy). The involvement of the skin, as the border site between clothes and the body, in the definition of dress troubles the delimitation of the body as the object that is to be dressed. This challenge to the very concept of the skin as bodily container is one pinpointed by the French psychoanalyst Eugénie Lemoine-Luccioni, whose book *La robe* was partly inspired by Orlan, and which contains a chapter on Orlan's pre-surgical work.[4] As Lemoine-Luccioni (1983: 98) puts it, "Once the skin is removed, there is no body left."[5] This insight—that the involvement of the skin in cultural practices (and in Orlan's case, in her surgical performances) challenges conventional definitions of dress *and* of the body—would seem to have implications for all art forms and practices—theater, performance, fashion—that can take the body as their object. Given its most radical interpretation, it completely rewrites the textuality of dress, allowing the body "itself" to be read as a kind of multilayered outfit of clothing. Printed on the sleeve of one of Orlan's assistants during one operation was the phrase "The body is but a costume."

Returning for a moment to the relationship of the skin to clothing proposed by Lemoine-Luccioni as an alternative to the familiar one, however, we can see that it neatly describes the crossover of the skin and dress that occurs in body-modification practices: "We prefer to consider the garment as equivalent to a second skin, and skin as equivalent to a sort of undergarment" (Lemoine-Luccioni 1983: 98). An inversion or invagination of this type is exactly what Orlan demonstrated in a performance in Lisbon in 1981, when she ran through crowded streets in an opaque black "chasuble" bearing a life-sized photographed print of her naked body. A policeman directing traffic who wanted to arrest her was persuaded by Orlan that there was nothing illegal about wearing such eye-catchingly printed clothing; it is, on the contrary, a mark of high fashion. Interestingly, the designer who has recently commercialized the printing of photographs onto separates in this way is Issey Miyake, who created the costumes for Orlan's 1993 operation/performance "Omnipresence." I recently saw a presenter on French television's cult Canal+ programme "Nulle part ailleurs" wearing a dress made by Miyake with a life-sized nude torso printed on it. With his autumn/winter 1995 collection Miyake broke new ground in the fashion establishment by showing his clothes on a group of women in their eighties: this versatility is an important part of his credo as a couturier, evidence of a democratic sensibility perhaps not immediately obvious in Orlan's exhibition of his gowns and hats in her work in the operating theatre (Frankel 1997: 14–19).

Despite mentioning the trope of invagination so strikingly illustrated by Orlan's Lisbon performance in her redefinition of the relationship of dress and the skin, Lemoine-Luccioni does not use it to advance questioning about the way it troubles the definition of the body. She does refer to the work of fellow-psychoanalyst Didier Anzieu, whose concept of the "Moi-peau" ("I-skin" or "ego-skin"), posits a coincidence of the child's developing ego with a "narcissistic envelope": "I employ the term I-skin to refer to a figuration used by the child's ego during the early stages of its development to represent itself as an ego containing psychic contents, on the basis of its experience of the body's surface" (Anzieu 1995: 61). Anzieu's concept of the "Moi-peau" radicalizes the importance of the projection of bodily surfaces to the formation of the ego seen in Freud's "bodily ego" and in Lacan's concept of the imaginary. The incorporation of the skin as organ of sensibility into ego-formation suggests the ego is a more sensitive and more fragile entity than it is often considered to be. But for Anzieu the skin appears to function as a bodily container whose boundaries are not put into question; the concept "Moi-peau" implies a coincidence of the limits of the body and the limits of the ego.

Lemoine-Luccioni (1983: 95) does, however, comment on the implication of the skin in questions of being: "Skin is disappointing [. . .] But it does nonetheless suggest something to do with being." In a formulation of which part is cited by Orlan at the beginning of all her performances, she continues (1983: 95):

> It is quite clear that the only possession he has ("my skin is all I have to my name" is a common expression) weighs heavily on him. It is still in excess, because having and being do not coincide, and because having is a cause of misunderstanding in all human relationships: I have the skin of an angel but I am a jackal, the skin of a crocodile, but I am a dog; a black skin but I am white; the skin of a woman but I am a man. I never have the skin of what I am. There is no exception to the rule because I am never what I have.

The skin pinpoints the disjuncture between having and being that occurs in Georg Simmel's reflections on adornment. If skin did not figure in analyses of dress during the stage of modernity commented on by Simmel, it does in the 1990s.

In the final chapter of *La robe* devoted to Orlan, Lemoine-Luccioni (1983: 137) returns to the question of the closure of the body, stating "The body is not closed. Nor is the garment which envelops it." Orlan's interest is not in weaving (that most archetypally feminine of activities) and the texturing of surfaces; she is more concerned with the opposite operations of rupturing and opening apparently hermetic wrappings and coverings: "Orlan un-weaves; she lacerates every enveloping layer" (1983: 143). This is most dramatically applied to the skin in Orlan's surgical work, but has also featured in her "living sculptures." In the first part of the Saint Theresa action, of which different "tableaux" were photographed for use in subsequent artworks, Orlan's breast emerged to be brandished from within the ornate drapery of her robes. (The second part of the action was more overtly destructive, including the cutting of the *drapé* into rags.) Amidst echoes of theatrical statues magically coming to life Orlan at a stroke pinpoints the specificity of performance and rebels against the passivity and chastity of an objectified subject of classical art history. The actions of opening and cutting she performs here with costume have been developed and radicalized in the surgical project "The Reincarnation of Saint Orlan." In the exhibition "Between Two," which recently toured the UK, there is a barely suppressed jubilation in the words accompanying the enlarged photo-plate of Orlan's face being cut away from the side of her head, "The body is open . . . ."

Woman in Space: Variations on Containment

In this final section I would like to return to the notion of the body as container, and consider it more closely, by first discussing a series of Orlan's performances that preceded "The Reincarnation of Saint Orlan." Dress again figures centrally in these performances, which are the *mesurages* or measurings first executed by Orlan in 1976 in Nice, and subsequently in 1977 at the Centre Georges Pompidou, in 1978 in Strasburg, and in 1979 in Lyons, at a festival of performance art organized by Orlan and Hubert Besacier. Further measurings took place at the Guggenheim Museum in New York in 1983, and again at the Centre Georges Pompidou in 1984 (Sarah Wilson 1996/7: 11–12).

What Orlan is doing when she places her body into a specific environment as a measure can be seen as an instance or citation of the science of anthropometry, which is a science consisting of the collection of the measurements of different human bodies for use by professional engineers and designers. According to Anne Balsamo, a feminist commentator on technology and the gendered body, anthropometry is a field with which many cosmetic surgeons have some familiarity, because of its interest in the establishment of ideals and norms of measurement which can then be used for the purposes of design. Balsamo (1996: 59) explains:

> Of course it makes a great deal of sense that measurement standards and scales of human proportions are a necessary resource for the design of products for human use; in order to achieve a "fit" with the range of products from office chairs to office buildings, designers must have access to a reliable and standardized set of body measurements.

The parallel of Orlan's measurings with the practice of anthropometry brings out two aspects of her actions. The first is that her body is female, and that its use as a measure is already different from the use of the male body which has traditionally lain behind the construction of systems of measurement. Some measures, such as the foot (and other less common ones such as the cubit, which is equivalent to the length of the forearm) are so familiar that we tend to forget that they are based on the male and not the female body. Orlan's use of her woman's body as a measure cannot contribute to the imagining of universals that take the male body as a norm. Instead, her actions suggest that she envisages a different, female universal—and that there should be, effectively, a double universal, as in the thinking of Luce Irigaray (cf. esp. 1992). Orlan's measurings should perhaps be described as the practice of *gyn*ometry rather than of anthropometry, a substitution of femaleness for maleness that highlights the gendered nature of a subject of (practical) science too often and for too long assumed to be "neutral," or free of the fundamental bodily modifiers of gender and race.

There is a striking affinity between Orlan's measurings and the reflections on the relationship of gender to the use of the body in space made by Christine Battersby (1993), in her article "Her Body/Her Boundaries." Within this larger problematic, the specific issues Battersby investigates are containment and bodily boundaries, and she mentions fashion and cosmetic surgery as highly significant methods by which women may discipline the boundaries of their bodies (1993: 33). Battersby's focus, however, is the idea of the body as a container for the inner self, an idea that she finds radically foreign to her own (female) experience of what it is to inhabit a body. Seeking an alternative to the view that envisages the body as "a container in which the self is inside and protected from the other by boundaries which protect against and resist external forces, whilst also holding back internal forces from expansion," Battersby turns not to a poststructuralist deconstruction of borders, but to "a metaphysics revisited from the perspective of gender—in order to reconstitute the inside/outside, self/other, body/mind divides [. . .] The move into feminist metaphysics opens up other possibilities which allow us to theorize a "real" *beyond* the universals of an imagination or a language which takes the male body and mind as ideal and/or norm" (1993: 32).

One alternative Battersby suggests to the experience of the female body as container—which she maintains may not be a typically female experience—is that "I [speaking as a woman] construct a containing space around me, precisely because my body itself is not constructed as the container" (1993: 34). The choice of enclosing architecture as the environment of Orlan's measurings indicates that what is going on is very akin to this construction of an extra-bodily container. Whilst the performance of the action of measuring in art galleries and other art spaces may be seen as a relatively straightforward claim upon those spaces by a woman artist, the choice of an ecclesiastical edifice for a measuring, in the case of the Musée St-Pierre in Lyons, a former monastery, can be read both as an assertion of the identity of "Saint Orlan" and as the appropriation of a space heavily imbued with the history and imagery of the established patriarchal Church.

Battersby ends "Her Body/Her Boundaries" by specifying that the new feminist metaphysics she is calling for "will not appeal to an unsymbolized imaginary" (1993: 38). This introduces the final idea I would like to focus on here, which is the idea of the female imaginary, in relation both to Orlan's work with dress and use of her body in space.

Twentieth-century philosophy offers a number of different theorizations of the imaginary. An extremely lucid summary and comparison of these is given by Margaret Whitford in her study of Luce Irigaray (Whitford 1991: Ch. 3). According to Whitford, one major source for the notion of the imaginary is phenomenology ("according to Sartre's definition, the imaginary is the intentional object of the *imagining* consciousness" (1991: 54)), and another the work of the French philosopher Gaston Bachelard, for whom the imaginary is also a function of the imagination. Perhaps the dominant theorization of the imaginary in recent years, however, has been the Lacanian one. Lacan's concept of the imaginary is related to his highly influential concept of the mirror stage, according to which a child's first glimpse of a unified image of its body is a key moment in the formation of its identity. Whereas the mirror stage describes a particular moment in childhood development, the imaginary designates an entire order that overlaps with the pre-Oedipal mirror stage, but also describes subsequent operations of the ego, such as identification and falling in love. Although the imaginary is a concept particular to Lacan, and not formulated as such by Freud, the role of the body-image in its formation has striking similarities with Freud's notion that the mental projection of bodily surfaces contributes significantly to the formation of the ego.

One idea that follows from the psychoanalytic conception of the imaginary in particular is that it (the imaginary) revolves around the role of the *specular image* in mental life. Since this image is based upon the outline or "envelope" of the body, dress, as well as body shape, will play a vital part in imaginary formations. Furthermore, the work of psychoanalysts has revealed that the limits of the body as perceived by the subject can undergo displacement, so that spaces to which the subject feels connected, such as its home, or a particular room in that home, act as extensions of its body image, and are as actively involved in the imaginary as the (dressed or undressed) profile of the body. This imaginary interplay of specular self-image, dress, and inhabited space, noted by Eugénie Lemoine-Luccioni at several points in *La robe*,[6] indicates a way of associating them different from those mentioned hitherto, and one that is highly suggestive where Orlan's work with all three "envelopes" is concerned.

The theorist of the imaginary Whitford herself is interested in is, of course, Luce Irigaray. Whitford explains Irigaray's imaginary as follows: "[Irigaray] conflates in a single term the phenomenological definition of the imaginary (the conscious, imagining and imaging mind) with the psychoanalytic definition (the unconscious, phantasying mind) and can move fluidly between one and the other" (1991: 54).

Another thinker of the imaginary with whom Irigaray has much in common is Cornelius Castoriadis, who, in addition to formulating a critique of Lacan's definition of the term, "deploys the concept of the imaginary in an explicit attempt to understand the persistence of social formations and the possibility of changing them" (Whitford 1991: 56). Like Irigaray, Castoriadis employs the term "imaginary" to describe both a primary creative force in the mind (conscious or unconscious), and a social formation. However, the last important feature of Irigaray's imaginary distinguishes her from Castoriadis too. This is that for Irigaray, the imaginary is sexuate [*sexué*]; in other words, it becomes meaningful to speak of a male and a female imaginary respectively, because the imaginary bears the morphological marks of the gendered body. The body that shapes the social imaginary is not an empirical but already a symbolic one, in which a metaphorical relationship to anatomy lends particular shape-related values to thought and to culture. This enables Irigaray to argue that Western patriarchal culture is and always has been shaped by the male imaginary, meaning that its cultural products carry the characteristics of male morphology—unity, linearity and closure. The traditional dominance of the male imaginary means that the female imaginary has been suppressed and not thoroughly theorized. Several definitions of it remain possible, however, all of which are characterized by fragmentation, fluidity, and openness (and there are important similarities here between Irigaray and the "new topologies" cited by Battersby as important to her new metaphysics of boundaries, whose basic paradigms would be those of potentialities, flow and permeability). Whitford is careful to point out that these descriptions of the female imaginary should not be read in an essentialist manner, but "as a description of the female as she appears in, and is symbolized by, the western cultural imaginary" (1991: 60).

Returning to Battersby's wish to avoid appealing to an unsymbolized imaginary, the process of undergoing analysis, in which diverse psychic material not previously dealt with by the subject is expressed in language or represented (symbolized) in some other way, can be described as a process of symbolization. However, if the imaginary is considered as a social concept, the issue of the unsymbolized imaginary has more far-reaching ramifications. It suggests that the feminine as a category is consigned to unmodifiable "dereliction" within the symbolic order, unless it can be re-symbolized within that order, a transformation of the conditions of representation as they relate to sexual difference.

I would like to suggest that in Orlan's work, both approaches to the imaginary are relevant, but that the latter is much more pertinent to those of her actions that revolve principally around dress and the use of her body in space. In other words, I do not want to exclude the consideration of Orlan as a psychoanalytic "case," whose singular relationship to the symbolic order may be being seen (and may even be being worked through) in her performance projects. This is an approach to her work that has already been taken and that yields fascinating observations.[7] But despite the interest of this deployment of the imaginary/symbolic relationship in relation to her work, the Irigarayan insistence on the gendered and social character of the imaginary, and its potential for social and political transformation, seems to me to offer a much readier reading of actions such as her public measurings. This is simply because the representations of which these actions consist are (always) already thoroughly public, thoroughly social. In the instance of Orlan's use of her body as a measure, the emphasis may be seen to be upon the visibility of a solitary woman's body in a public space, a representation that emphasizes her femaleness, and implicitly comments upon the gender-bias both of systems of measurement and of the differing relationships of the two sexes to geometry, architecture, design, and space.

A further aspect of Orlan's measurings has even more striking resonances with the definitions of the female imaginary offered by Irigaray. This is the ritual washing of the clothes worn by Orlan during the performance, which also takes place in public. The dirty water left over from this washing is then placed in sealed jars as "relics" of Saint Orlan, a procedure also used with flesh extracted from Orlan's body by liposuction in "The Reincarnation of Saint Orlan":

> The "maculae," stains, the sweat and dust-infused water [. . .] was collected in a bowl and then transferred to containers sealed with wax as relics. The Virgin, conceived "immaculately," without stain, counters the tradition of the bride's display of bloodied linen after the wedding night . . . . [Orlan's] "measuring" performances

Figure 3
"Orlan-body," Measuring of an Institution, Musée St. Pierre, Lyons, 1979.
(Photo SIPA Press, Paris).

> provoked violently sexual reactions: she was spat upon, insulted as "a woman of the streets"; the trial of measurement passes through filth (Wilson 1996/7: 11–12).

In this way residual traces of the contact of Orlan's clothing with her body and with the environment are preserved, traces that could be seen as emblematic of the "scraps" and "debris" characteristic of an emergent, alternative female imaginary, as sketched out by Irigaray (Whitford 1991: 59, 67). Another account of the measuring that took place at the Musée St-Pierre in Lyons in 1979 reveals that chalk-markings made by Orlan of each re-positioning of her body in the measuring constitute another trace of the unfamiliar passage of a female body through a space whose architecture and form (a quadrangle of cloisters) connotes predominantly the closure and unity of patriarchal representation (*Premier Symposium International d'Art Performance de Lyon* 1980). This account also describes the vigor with which Orlan carries out the washing of her clothes, described as "an act of pressure," and the quasi-jubilation she shows after exerting this effort. This energy put by Orlan into the act of preserving representations of the contact of her body with the environment is suggestive of the kind of "excess" Irigaray also associates with a female imaginary that "jams the machinery" of patriarchal representation and can be seen seeking alternative forms, or alternatives to the traditional conception of "form" itself.

An unquestioned assumption of much work in performance is that the body constitutes the "theatrical" object *par excellence*. One aim of my study of Orlan's work is to investigate the possibility that she is undoing the very notion of the body as aesthetic object as often assumed in performance and theater. A number of other performance artists, such as Stelarc and Marina Abramovic, have done or are currently doing work that also focuses on the skin, and the question of whether the body can or should be thought of as a container, and by focusing on dress, the skin and the definition of the body, Orlan's artistic practice constantly raises and dramatizes similar issues. As I have suggested by drawing on the ideas of Irigaray and Christine Battersby, a reformulation of the problem of bodily boundaries and the body in space is most usefully approached via a parallel discussion of gender difference. Irigaray's concept of the female imaginary claims dynamic and transformative potential for symbolic practice involving the female body. A reminder of some words of Orlan's about her work as a woman artist is timely at this point: "Art can, art *must* change the world, it's its only justification."[8]

Notes

1. These include "One-off striptease with trousseau sheets," performed in Lyons in 1976, "Drapery—the Baroque," done in Venice in 1979, and "Mise-en scène pour une sainte," again in Lyons in 1981.
2. Orlan actually refers to her practice not as "body art," but as "carnal art," to distinguish it from the work of the late 1960s and early 1970s founding generation of body artists (Gina Pane, Chris Burden, Vito Acconci *et al.*).
3. The material summarized in this paragraph is drawn from Linda Grant (1995).
4. Lemoine-Luccioni says of the genesis of her book, in the preface (1983: 7), "Then Monique Veaute introduced me to Orlan, and I knew from the start where my own enquiry would lead me."
5. Lemoine-Luccioni 1983: 98. All translations from this and other French publications are my own.
6. "At the moment when specular experience began, when his image appeared in the mirror under the active guarantee of the mother's look, he gave himself a frame. This specular image, which in Lacanian algebra is written i (o), is man's first garment" (Lemoine-Luccioni 1983: 78). Further references are p. 82, p. 90 (in the chapter "Image spéculaire—vêtement—maison"), p. 111.
7. *VST: revue scientifique et culturelle de santé mentale*, 23/24, Sept.–Dec. 1991. This issue is devoted entirely to Orlan.
8. Orlan, "Conférence," in *Ceci est mon corps . . . ceci est mon logiciel/ This is my body . . . this is my software*, 1996/7: 85.

References

Anzieu, Didier 1995 [1985]. *Le Moi-peau*, 2nd edn, Paris: Dunod. (First edn Paris: Bordas, 1985).

Balsamo, Anne 1996. *Technologies of the Gendered Body: Reading Cyborg Women*. Durham: Duke University Press.

Battersby, Christine 1993. "Her Body/Her Boundaries: Gender and the Metaphysics of Containment," *Journal of Philosophy and the Visual Arts*, ed. Andrew Benjamin, 1993: 30–9.

Ceci est mon corps . . . ceci est mon logiciel/This is my body . . . this is my software 1996/7. Catalogue to the exhibition of plates from "Omnipresence," shown Newcastle, Edinburgh and London, UK, 1996/7.

Frankel, Susannah 1997. "Between the Pleats," *The Guardian Weekend*, 19 July 1997, pp. 14–19.

Grant, Linda 1995. "Written on the Body," *The Guardian Weekend*, 1 April 1995, pp. 12–20.

Irigaray, Luce 1984. "La différence sexuelle." in *Ethique de la différence sexuelle*, Paris: Editions de Minuit.

—— 1992. *J'aime à toi*, Paris: Editions Grasset & Fasquelle.

Lemoine-Luccioni, Eugénie 1983. *La Robe: essai psychoanalytique sur le vêtement*, Paris: Editions du Seuil.

McClellan, Jim 1994. "The Extensions of Woman," *The Observer "Life" Magazine*, 17 April 1994, pp. 38–42.

Premier Symposium International d'Art Performance de Lyon 1980. Lyons: Editions du Cirque Divers.

Rose, Barbara 1993. "Is It Art? Orlan and the Transgressive Act," *Art in America*, February 1993, pp. 82–7, 125.

Simmel, Georg 1985. "Adornment," Epigraph to Elizabeth Wilson, *Adorned in Dreams: Fashion and Modernity*, London: Virago.

VST: revue scientifique et culturelle de santé mentale 1991. [Orlan issue], 23/24, Sept.–Dec. 1991.

Whitford, Margaret 1991. *Luce Irigaray: Philosophy in the Feminine*, London: Routledge.

Wilson, Elizabeth 1985. *Adorned in Dreams: Fashion and Modernity*, London: Virago.

Wilson, Sarah 1996/7. "L'histoire d'O, Sacred and Profane," in *Ceci est mon corps . . . ceci est mon logiciel/This is my body . . . this is my software*, Catalogue to the exhibition of plates from "Omnipresence," shown Newcastle, Edinburgh and London, UK, 1996/7, pp. 7–17.

Fashion Theory, Volume 2, Issue 2, pp.129–150
Reprints available directly from the Publishers.
Photocopying permitted by licence only.

Thinness and Other Refusals in Contemporary Fashion Advertisements

Katharine Wallerstein

Katharine Wallerstein received an M.A. from Duke University for work on French and American cultural history. She has written, taught, and spoken on style, sexuality, subcultural identity and advertising. She was curator of the *exhibit dadaism: Zurich, New York, Berlin, Paris* at Duke University.

Introduction

As an icon of fashion and popular culture in the 1990s, British supermodel Kate Moss has inspired both awe and harsh criticism. At once admired for being the working-class girl with just the right look who skyrocketed to fame as a top model, and reviled by critics for her ultra-thin, "waifish" figure and demeanor, Moss, along with the Calvin Klein ads in which she first appeared, has elicited an interesting and not altogether contradictory set of reactions. Kate Moss rose to fame as a model not by virtue of traditional high fashion glamour, but rather by virtue of her abject mien, distanced manner, and wan, androgynous look.

MATSUDA
YUKIO KOBAYASHI

From Calvin Klein's cK jeans advertisements of 1992, to the Obsession advertising campaigns of the subsequent few years, to the most recent for cK one cologne and cK be, Moss has commanded attention through her sullen, withdrawn demeanor and her streetwise, jaded airs. Her moody manner and rough-but-gentle appearance, combined with her skinny, tomboyish figure (in the earliest images she was barely 15)[1] have lent the various pictures in which she appeared a tone of ambiguity and androgyny, a sexual vagueness that seems intricately connected to her melancholic and detached affectations.

If in the early 1990s this new aesthetic in fashion advertising was primarily associated with Kate Moss and Calvin Klein, before long it had become a defining look in the designing, advertising, and photographing of fashion for companies and designer lines the world over, especially those geared toward a young, "hip," urban clientele. Advertisements for designer lines such as cK, Matsuda, Prada, Miu Miu, and Hugo, to name but a few, started featuring young models posed as alienated and disengaged, with numbed or depressed facial expressions and postures, often ultra-thin bodies, and at times distinctly unhealthy demeanors. Models have of course always been young, always been thin,[2] and have always affected detached, blasé poses. If there was something different in the new aesthetic, it was in the way it exaggerated these qualities that had always been part of fashion language. Suddenly, everyone was just a little *too* thin, or *too* pale. Detachment now bordered on depressed withdrawal. It is this deliberate dwelling in an aesthetic of thin, pale withdrawal, an aesthetic of abjection, that some people have found so disturbing.

This aesthetic has been attacked as an incitement to anorexia, as heroin chic, or simply as passive self-absorption. By contrast, I wish to suggest a more complicated reading of these ads. I would argue that the unwholesome look and disengaged poses of the models are in fact exceedingly passionate; that their thin, withdrawn bodies and melancholic demeanors enact not only emptiness, but a deliberate refusal to be filled, fulfilled, satisfied. I suggest that this look of hunger or unfulfillment denotes an intensity of emotion and experience; and that the refusal of fulfillment and the insistence on dwelling in a state of need and lack (whether lacking in food, in emotional nurturance, or in the completed process of socialization into categories of identity) suggests a counter-social, rebellious act. I suggest that this is a look whose roots reach far outside fashion advertising; that hunger, ailment, wanness and withdrawal have often been configured together in an aesthetic of passionate intensity. Examples of this can be seen in the cult of consumptive beauty in the nineteenth century; in the role that fasting and physical weakness has played in the attainment of higher spiritual or emotional states in numerous times and places; and in the enduring romantic figure, in literature, in art, and in our collective imagination, of the starving artist. It is this same intensity, I will suggest, that we find

Figure 1
Advertisement for Matsuda which appeared in *Vogue Homme International Mode, Automne/Hiver 94–95 – Hors Série*. Photo by Naka. © Matsuda.

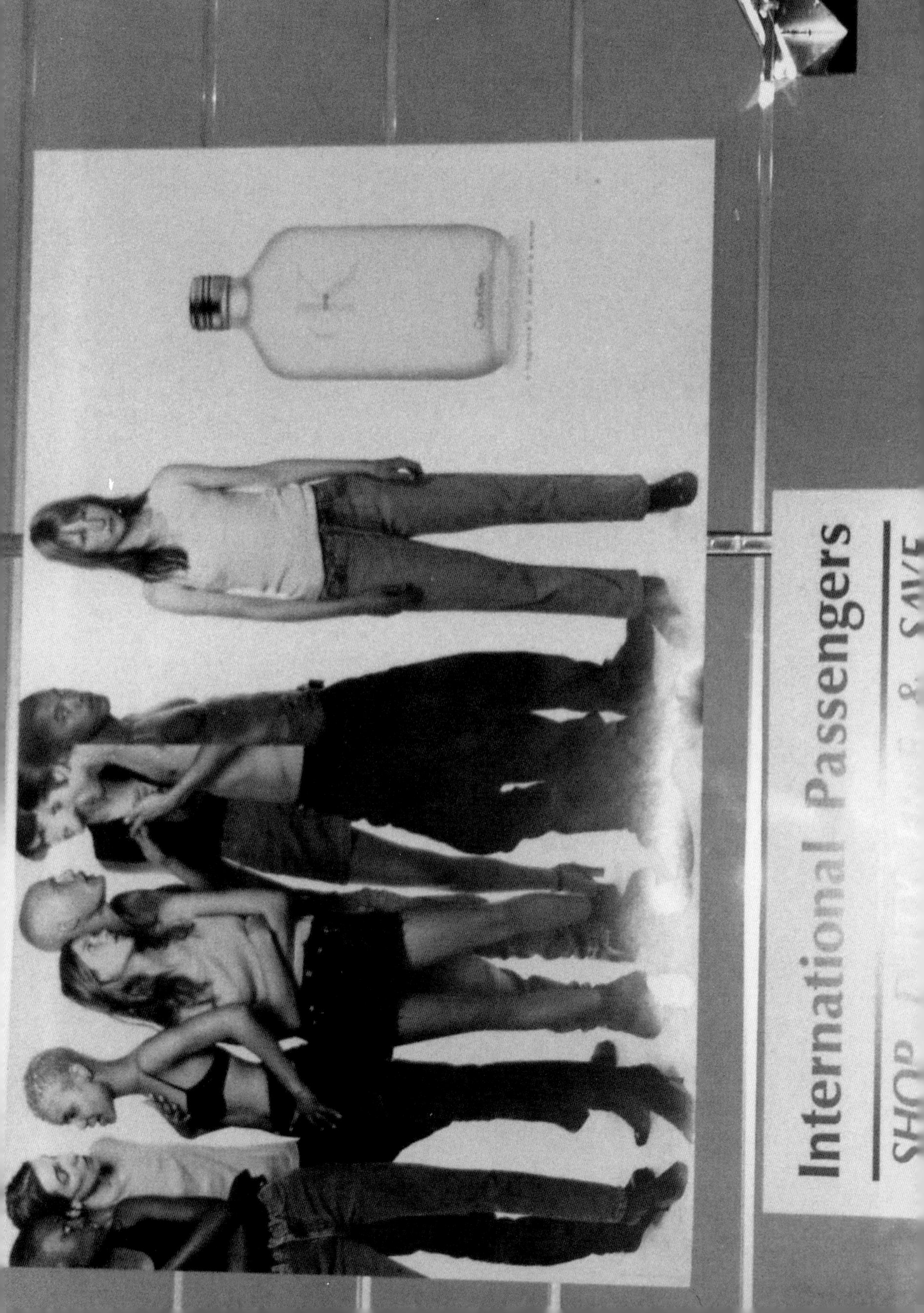
International Passengers

in these ads. Finally, I consider the part that black-and-white photography plays in the creation of this look in these ads today; that black-and-white is itself a withholding of color, of fullness and fulfillment. I suggest that these images capitalize on a language of documentary realism to create a drama of hunger, abjection, and lack.

Refusal, Unavailability, and Resistant Style in Recent Ads

I would like to begin by describing a few of these advertisements, at least some of which I hope will be familiar to the reader. First, in a number of early ads for Calvin Klein's cK jeans (starting in 1992) featuring Kate Moss, the model was posed to appear bored, disengaged, slightly pouty, and haughty in an adolescent kind of way. The photographs, almost always in black-and-white, were usually shot from below so as to emphasize her aloofness. In these ads, Moss wears the jeans that she is advertising, but she wears them low and baggy according to street style, and with gender-neutral and even masculine accessories: a simple tank top, a denim shirt attached by a single button revealing an almost flat chest, heavy black boots. She looks streetwise and tough, at once a kid and a young woman, dressed and posed with defiance. The drape of her clothes suggest a thin, lanky body, toughened and unnurtured, a body poised and ready to provoke.

My second example is a series of campaigns for Hugo Boss's secondary line Hugo (1995–7), which feature the James Dean-like anti-hero model Werner Schreyer. Schreyer, wearing a casual-chic Hugo suit and shirt, usually open at the neck with no tie, always appears slightly unkempt. His face, when we see it, displays a minimum of emotion. He is often looking at the ground, or else quite simply just walking away from the viewer. He, or the persona he enacts in the ad series, does not care much about us, or rather, he would have us believe that he is too wrapped up in his own boredom, or sluggishness to bother smiling or to stand up straight for the camera. The ads in this series are only faintly colored, suggesting a washed-out, aging photograph. These pictures are deliberately not bright, colorful, or vibrant. On the contrary, through the poses and affects of the models, and through the composition and style of the photograph, the images appear rather slow and depressed, suggesting a certain *angst*, as well as a non-conformist attitude.

Figure 2
Advertisement for cK one cologne on display at Pittsburg International Airport, August 1997.

A very similar series of ads for Pepe jeans appeared a few years before the Hugo campaign. This series featured Jason Priestley (star of the popular TV series, "90210")—again, a depressed (in these ads), hard-knocks, ruggedly handsome and brooding James Dean-like figure. These Pepe ads were designed to look like creased black-and-white images, suggesting magazine cut-outs, folded and stuck into the back pocket of someone's jeans. Again, the allure of these advertisements lay in their

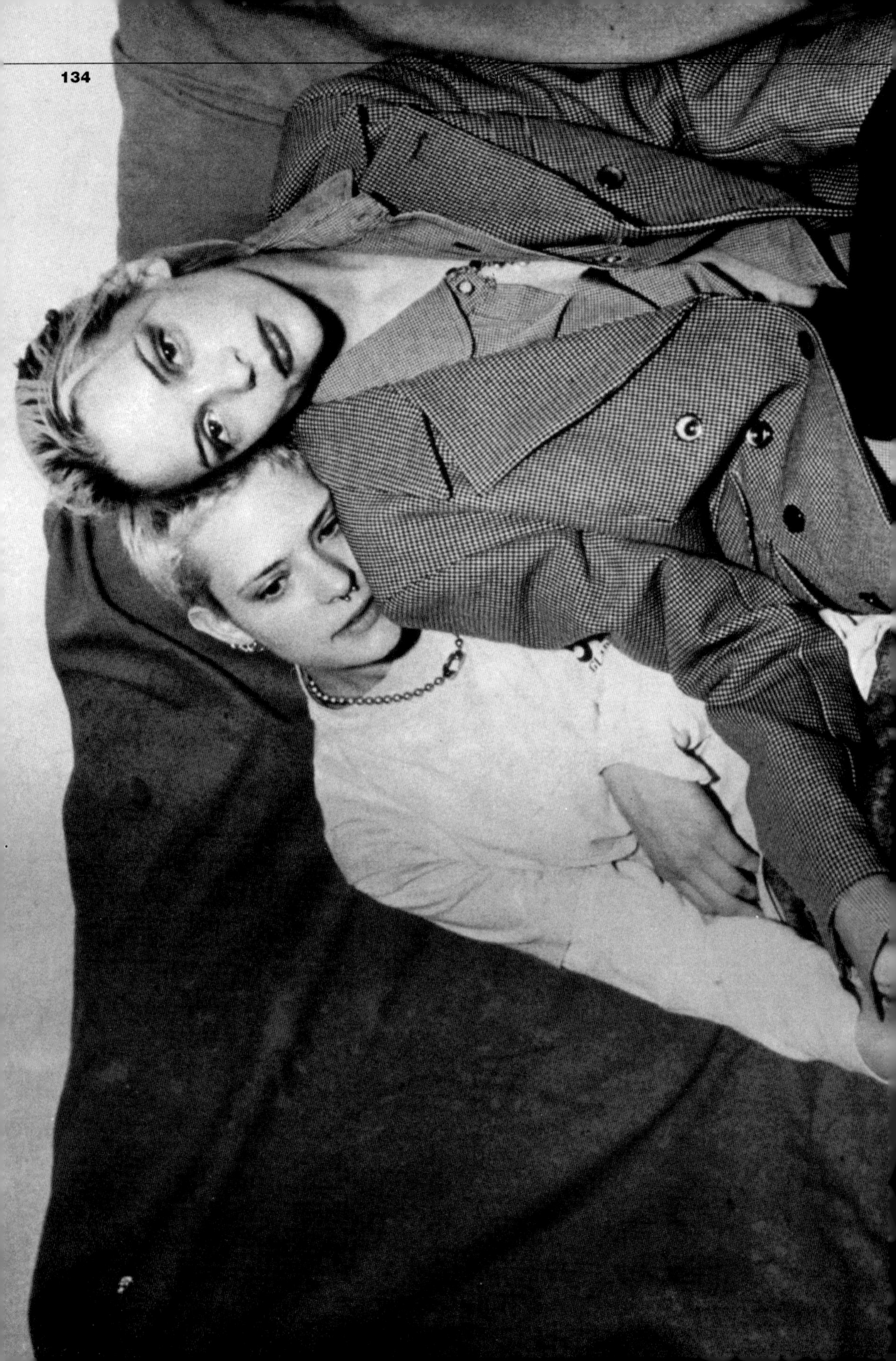

beat-up look, in their suggestion of careless, wandering young men, not quite living a responsible life, and not really trying to, either. Nothing in the Hugo or Pepe jeans ads is cheerful, enthusiastic, outgoing, or warm. On the contrary, the figures are inward-looking and seem to be carrying heavy burdens. Perhaps they have already seen too much; perhaps they understand, quite romantically, that the world is cruel and fragile, that the structures of stability meant to protect them are in fact vulnerable paper castles. Such, in any case, is the melodrama that one might envisage behind the pained and numbed expressions in the faces of these young figures.

This unhappy jadedness and dark emotional condition can be seen as well in ads for Matsuda. One such ad is set in what looks like a sparse, cold basement apartment (Figure 1). This ad features two ragged, artsy-looking young men, who appear jaded and fatigued, as if they've seen a lot, done a lot, flown high, and now are low. This sense of having *done* and *known* things, of having lived intensely and reached some kind of ecstatic height, is an essential part of this aesthetic, and appears time and again in these ads, in the form of burned-out, numbed expressions on the faces of the models, and in the renunciatory, lethargic postures of their bodies.

Finally, in recent (1997) ads for Prada, models are clad in tacky colors, their demeanor matching their clothes in pallor and in fatigue. These ads are dark, dirty, secretive, slightly menacing, and depressed. They also exude a brooding sexual energy, seen especially in the series featuring actor Joaquin Phoenix, and as well in the series with supermodel Amber Valletta. In one, for instance, she is reclining in a boat, looking right at us, her legs suggestively spread just a little, arm flung over her thin stomach, breasts outlined by the tightness of her young girl's dress. The setting is dark; everything seems under the shadow of night. Similarly recent ads for Miu Miu feature a young model not unlike the early Kate Moss, whose compellingly strange, beautiful, pouty, depressed look suggests at once loneliness, alienation, and unsociability, yet also an intensity of experience, emotion, and sexuality.

The sullen, dark, unhappy figures in these ads are, then, I would argue, quite passionate. Their dark emotions, erotic undertones, and intensities of expressions (even in their refusal of affect) suggest romantic notions of tragic beauty and ecstatic experiences achieved through physically destructive expenditures—such as drug-induced highs, sleep-deprived euphoria, famishment, or extreme emotional or physical experience. They seem to have "burned their candle at both ends." They look spent, exhausted from life and from living on the edge and in the margins, so that they can only express the intensity of what they've lived through a deliberate lack of affect.

Figure 3
Advertisement for Matsuda which appeared in *Interview*, August 1996. Photo by Nan Goldin. © Matsuda.

The emotionless emotion and passionate detachment that mark these figures have marked a variety of styles of dis-identification with dominant social systems in the history of counter-cultural and avant-garde expressions. This jaded, indifferent, seen-it-all, done-it-all look fills our literary and visual descriptions of world-weary rebels. It has resurfaced particularly in artistic and intellectual circles: think of nineteenth-century figures such as the dispassionate *flâneur*, the disdainful dandy, the *fumiste* bohemian affecting dramatic airs, the snobbish aesthete, the café-dweller, the student smoking and wearing black. Such poses have also figured centrally in numerous youth and counter-cultural styles that have emerged since the Second World War, particularly in Britain and in the United States, among groups such as mods, teddy boys, beatniks, hipsters, bikers, hippies, punks, dykes, queers, and so on and so forth. These figures and images constitute an aesthetic—and political—history, whose elements include disaffection, refusal, sexual ambiguity, and, most importantly, a cool distancing of the physical self and an aura of unavailability.

The affected and dispassionate styles of this study follow upon this history. They also, of course, take a particular shape as the product of our own times and subcultures. For instance, such styles take shape in the defiantly abject bodies of "generation x" slackers, in grunge, in skate culture, in tattoos and piercings, in gender-bendings, and in other "outlaw" cultural styles, all of which, taken together, constitute a complex of counter-social discourses out of which, and as part of which, the ads of this study emerge.

My point, however, in suggesting a continuity between "actual" resistant styles and fashion advertising is not to suggest that they have been "co-opted" by the media. Instead, I wish to place the productions of such styles on a cultural field which encompasses both the margins and the mainstream, or rather, to emphasize the fluidity, overlap, and dialogue between the two. Many critics object to what they see as the commercialization and depoliticization of fashions originating in street cultures and counter-cultures—the "mainstream" appropriation of hippy, of punk, of piercing and tattooing, of skate-kid-styled baggy jeans and oversized clothes, or of the blurring of sex and gender binaries by self-proclaimed queers and radicals. All of these are styles that have been represented in advertisements. Resistant style, as I understand it, is not born in one place, but is produced through dynamic interactions *across* and *between* various cultural fronts—subculture may feed the media, but the media have certainly fed subculture. I feel that it is limiting and often unproductive to try to demarcate one side of this exchange as authentic and original and the other as inauthentic and derivative. Such a linear interpretation of an inherently circular system of signification ignores the complexities of cultural production and subversive expression in a consumer culture whose economy of images is always already a commercial one. I wish the advertising images of this study, which I am arguing show resistant, refusing styles, to be understood not as copies of other more "real" versions of the same styles, but as expressions of a similar "truth" whose value lies not in its originality but in what it seeks to capture.

Hunger

One of the defining features of these ads is the extreme thinness of many of the models. Or, more accurately, if the models are not all extraordinarily thin (and not all are), still their appearances suggest a wasting and a wasted-ness. The two main objections that have been voiced in relation to this wave of fashion advertisements, in fact, have invoked just this: that the models are very thin, and that they look as though they're on drugs. I would like to suggest a reading of these bodies that reiterates elements of these interpretations, but that carries them toward a substantially different conclusion.

The significance of thinness, in the images of models such as Kate Moss, has been both oversimplified and underestimated. Thinness, historically and today, has had a much more complex and varying signification than is allowed for in the standard critiques of "waif" models (critiques that seek to implicate fashion models' thin bodies as a contributing cause to an epidemic of anorexia and other eating disorders, primarily but not exclusively among adolescent girls). Achieving thinness of body, or dwelling in a state of slight hunger, has been, in various times and places and in various different circumstances, for women as well as for men, a form of control and of strength. For instance, fasting, in many religions, is necessary to achieving a heightened spiritual or contemplative state. Fasting for any number of reasons can bring one to intense physical and spiritual heights. Maud Ellmann, in her book on the subject of self-starvation, *The Hunger Artists: Starving, Writing, and Imprisonment*, suggests that "self-inflicted hunger is a struggle to release the body from all contexts, even from the context of embodiment itself. It de-historicizes, de-socializes, and even de-genders the body" (Ellmann 1993: 14). Thinness and self-inflicted hunger, even within the domain of fashion today, can have a variety of overlapping meanings. In other words, the thin, weakened body does not always, or *only*, signify a subordinated body (as many critics have suggested); it can also signify, for instance, a disciplined body, a self-possessed body, a body in search of states of intensity, and a defiant body.

There is, of course, a significant history to thinness in the fashion world. Over the course of this century, thin, lanky, androgynous bodies, poised and detached with exaggerated disaffection, have repeatedly appeared in the advertising, selling, and performance of fashion. In the 1920s, for instance, absurdly elongated, detached, and jaded-looking figures—both men and women—dominated magazine illustrations and fashion plates. If we were to compare the posture and over-all affect of a typical art deco 1920s fashion plate to a 1990s Kate Moss ad, we would note some remarkable similarities. In both, we find models arranged in the same aloof poses, the hip jutted, the head slightly cocked, the look disengaged and jaded. Both would be marked by extreme exaggeration, the one through the medium of illustration, the other through the deliberateness of the photographed pose. Elongated thinness, removal, and disaffection have pervaded twentieth-century fashion, whether in the 1920s or today, whether haute couture and classic, or trendy and ready-to-wear. Removal and disaffection have been bound to thinness in the lexicon of twentieth-century fashion imagery. The exaggeratedly thin and androgynous bodies of models such as Kate Moss must be seen, I would suggest, against this history of thinness as a signifier of removal and disaffection in the language of fashion.

How does thinness evoke removal? On a literal level, the thin body, unencumbered by weight, curves, or bulk, can slip by unnoticed and without a trace; in other words, it can make itself less present. Furthermore, the streamlined androgynous body is a simplified body, divested of complications and metaphorically free of frills. Through its simplified, unencumbered, and flexible disposition, the thin body allows for the lanky, curved or sunken pose that has been so prevalent in twentieth-century fashion. Such a pose, or stance, emphasizes the distance assumed by the figure, the removal of the thin, wispy figure, which is *not* standing to attention. Thinness can thus be said to signify removal.

Of course, thinness also signifies hunger. Hunger is often associated with a lack of food, but may also be associated with a refusal to eat: a refusal of food and nourishment but also, more broadly, of nurturance and softness. A hungry body is also, importantly, an abject body. To be abject, according to the OED, is to be "Cast off, rejected . . . self-abasing." An abject body, as I am using it here, is one that goes against standards of acceptability; one that is sickly, unhealthy, or outcast, and deliberately so. In her essay on abjection, Julia Kristeva discusses the significance of the refusal of food, stating that "food loathing is perhaps the most elementary and most archaic form of abjection." The refusal of food, she explains, signifies the separation of the child from the parents who want to nourish it (Kristeva 1982: 2). Such a refusal of nourishment can be clearly seen in the Matsuda ad of Figure 1. The figure in the rear of the image is holding a bottle of milk—a symbol of health, purity, and nurturance. Though the act of holding the milk indicates an intent to drink it, in the picture he is simply standing there, thin, withdrawn, a little out-of-it, with the milk bottle in hand. The juxtaposition of the white, nourishing milk with his under-nourished-looking body and burned-out look is striking. The bottle of milk remains in his hand; he seems suspended in that moment of need, but in no hurry to satisfy the need. And indeed he does not look dissatisfied. His gaze is dreamy and glazed, his mouth is slightly, sensuously, ajar. Perhaps he will not drink the milk at all. One can easily imagine him lighting up a cigarette instead: smoking endlessly, sustaining himself on cigarettes and black coffee, perhaps thinking occasionally about food, but not doing much more than that. He feeds on nothingness, one imagines, and sustains himself, like a true starving artist, musician, or bohemian, *through* such hungry emptiness.

The link between hunger and creativity has endlessly filled romantic images and descriptions of the artistic process. The figure of the starving artist or of the starving writer reappears with every generation of avant-gardists, artists, and intellectuals of all sorts. In a short story called "Hunger Was a Good Discipline," Ernest Hemingway writes of a time he spent in Paris, with little money or food. He speaks of going to the Luxembourg Museum, where "all the paintings were sharpened and clearer and more beautiful if you were belly-empty, hollow-hungry. I learned to understand Cezanne much better," he wrote, "and to see truly how he made landscapes when I was hungry" (Hemingway 1990: 416). "Hunger is good discipline", he tells us, "and you learn from it" (Hemingway 1990: 418). Almost a century earlier, Rimbaud declared that he had lost his taste for any food but earth and stones. Commenting on Rimbaud's '*fêtes de la faim*' (festivals of hunger/feasts of famine), Ellmann writes that "To write, for Rimbaud, is to hunger, and it is only through a diet of stone-crop that the poet can accede to the inhuman solitude of art. This visionary hunger also resembles the miraculous abstinence of the medieval saints, for whom to fast was not to overcome the flesh so much as to explore the limits of corporeality, where humanity surrenders to a bodiliness so extreme that it coalesces with the bestial or divine" (Ellmann 1993: 13). The experience of the hungering body, of suspended pleasure, of un-fulfillment, of non-consummation sharpens perceptions and engenders creativity. Hunger feeds the senses.

Hunger and unfulfillment have long been associated with passionate experience and with some sense of living outside the normative or material world. Hungry, physically needing bodies, a look of ill health, and attraction to that which will destroy health and create ecstatic hunger and emptiness, such as drugs, cigarettes,[3] or starvation, have gone together to dramatic and rebellious effect: from the romanticization of consumption and the fetishization of pale, anemic, tubercular bodies in the nineteenth century;[4] to the emergent figure in the same era of the struggling artist, feverishly and heroically producing unrecognized masterpieces from the afflicted spaces of poverty and hunger; to the angry, brutalized bodies of 1970s and 1980s punk and the ragged, unkempt styles of 1990s grunge; to drug cultures of different eras - opium, or absinthe (the artist's drug of choice in the nineteenth century),[5] or hallucinogenics and heroin today. The air of drug-induced lethargy or dreaminess, or the burned-out look of some of the figures in these ads, which has drawn much criticism in 1997, needs to be considered in the light of this link between unhealthy and other-worldly physical states and alternative and oppositional cultural positions. In a May 1997 op-ed piece in the *New York Times* responding to the outrage surrounding "heroin chic," author Linda Yablonsky argued that there is something attractive as well as mysterious about the junkie look. "Most heroin addicts I knew wanted a wasted appearance" she said. "They were quite vain about it." "Drugs give them a certain arrogance: They think they feel better than we do, that they know something we don't" (Yablonsky 1997: 15). Yablonsky suggests that the mystery created by that attitude is what fashion photos try to evoke. The romance of altered states, that sense of having gone somewhere *else*—away from this mundane, limiting, material world—is what makes this look so captivating. Speaking of the link between writing and starving, Ellmann states that "we do not starve to write, but write to starve: and we starve in order to affirm *the supremacy of lack*, and to extend the ravenous dominion of the night" (Ellmann 1993: 27; italics mine). That look of hunger, of aching emptiness, that look of having been up all night, of feverish fatigue, of having flirted with danger, with death, a look associated with drugs, with fasting, with sex, with intense emotional experiences, and with the dangerous excitement of the night, speaks of the highest experience of living. There is a purity to the experience of being so close to the edge, to being almost not there any more, a transcendent experience to being, as Emily Dickinson described her experience of fasting, "inebriate of air" (Ellmann 1993: 2). In their unfed and burned-out demeanors, these figures suggest such experiences.

The thin body, then, is one that refuses to nourish itself, to fill itself out, to be present. In refusing the physical, however, the thin, abject body draws attention to the physical, to the body, to its emotional presence, to its sexuality (which is related to nourishment), to its emptiness. A television ad for Boston Market restaurant that ran in the summer of 1997 did a wonderful parody of this emptiness. In the ad, we see several slacker figures in black and white who are clearly made to resemble figures from various cK and Obsession ads languishing on a rock by a beach (an Obsession ad reference). A voice-over whispers "Emptiness. Emptiness. How can I fill this empty void of emptiness?" Immediately, a healthy-bodied, ruddy-complexioned adult appears in color and tells the kids "It's not tricky. Eat something. Trust me. Eating is a good thing"—at which point they, still in black and white, follow him to Boston Market, where they will eat, be filled, and, presumably, come into color. This ad cleverly identifies the discourse of emptiness that is going on in ads such as cK one and Obsession, and names that emptiness as at once physical (these dieting, careless, waif-like adolescents need to eat some meat) and emotional (they are wistful teens, immersed in their *angst*, boredom, and feelings of futility). But while extremely insightful, what this ad misses is that the body that refuses to nourish itself, to fill itself out, to be present, is not a passive body like the figures in the ad, who are quickly and easily persuaded by the colorful man to abandon their dark moods and empty stomachs, but is instead a purposeful, confrontational, assertive body.

The thin body in fact announces itself in the negative; it asserts its presence through a physical and emotional removal, or disengagement, and by denying itself the fulfillment of nurturance. These bodies confront not only through denying their own nurturance, but, moreover, through denying their availability. Looking at the figures in these ads, one of the first things that one notices, along with their thin, withdrawn look, is their lack of smiles. The unsmiling model is nothing new to fashion. She, or he, has signaled seriousness, stylishness, and seduction. What is striking about the unsmiling models in the advertising images of today is their lack of *any* pretense to pleasantness or openness. Not only are they not smiling, they are resolutely not smiling. They are assaulting in their unsmilingness, willfully refusing expected codes of social interaction, codes that dictate openness and availability. These figures announce their unavailability through their unsmiling faces, just as much as through their hungering thinness, withdrawn postures, and removed airs. In one of a series of 1994 Obsession magazine ads, for instance, a topless Kate Moss looks at the camera, her hand covering her mouth (and not her breasts), a wisp of hair blowing across her face. It is unusual to see a bare-breasted woman at the center of an advertisement. Yet, to invoke John Berger's classic distinction, if Moss appears naked (without clothes), she is not nude (a sexualized object of our gaze) (Berger 1972)—at least not in the classic sense in which nudity, or the hint of nudity, might be used in an advertisement. For what is striking about this ad is not her nakedness, but the slightly strange and disturbed manner in which it is presented to us. Moss appears wasted, bony, bleached, anemic, more like the sickly consumptive of nineteenth-century literature than a tantalizing model. Her pale, ghostly demeanor makes her seem physically unavailable to us, her small breasts and rigid torso only adding an element of mystery and inaccessibility to the picture (is she a woman? a child? a boy?). Moss is alone, beyond reach, and yet, at the same time, extraordinarily present. She asserts her presence through her unavailability. She confronts through her withdrawal.

Incompletion

The unsmiling, withdrawn thinness that we see in these ads signifies the rejection of dominant codes of social interaction, namely *availability*,[6] and the refusal of acceptable bodily norms. Such norms, as I have just discussed, dictate that a body be nourished, that it strive (even if it does not succeed) to be happy, "open" or available in body language. They dictate as well that a body present itself and maintain its status as one of two clearly identifiable genders—male or female. The refusal of such social imperatives is a rejection of those social orders and regulatory regimes that dictate those norms, and that socialize, or nurture, the subject to act in certain ways. And if the "success" of these regimes depends on, and is in fact epitomized by, the socialization of the child into an adult—a strong, rational, mature, fully socialized figure who has been successfully nurtured to the point of being able to nurture others—then central to what is going on in these representations is the refusal of adulthood.

Thinness that results not only in the unsmiling, thin, unhealthy body, but also in fact in the androgynous body, can be said to be not only the refusal of adulthood in general—of its responsibility, its rationality, and its dicta on convention and normality—but also of the adult body itself. The refusal of the adult body signifies the refusal of the fully developed sexed body, or of a body that has reached completion as either male or female, that is, man or woman, and, conjointly, as either heterosexual or homosexual.

One trend in which this willed incompletion has been clearly manifest is in the numerous ads that feature young women wearing babydoll dresses, in sexually provocative poses that nonetheless mimic the pose of a child or young adolescent who is still "innocently" unaware of proper adult body language. One such ad for Katharine Hamnett, photographed by Juergen Teller, shows a girl, probably in her teens, leaning back on a rock, legs dangling beneath her short dress, so short that it is rising to expose—almost—her underwear, just as a child's short dress might expose her still "innocent" pubic area. In an essay on fashions of "outgrown clothes for grown-up people," Lee Wright suggests that "smallness creates an impression of a garment in the process of being outgrown" (Wright 1992: 40). The smallness of the "babydoll" dress, literally modeled after a little girl's dress, when worn by a grown woman, as in the style of the mid-1990s, suggests both a confusion of age (is the person wearing the dress a woman or a child?) and a throwback to the excited suspension of that moment right before adolescence, when the body is on the cusp of sexual definition, but can still get away with being that of a child. The little girl dress on the young woman's body suggests a child's body being outgrown by a maturing, more sexually adult figure. The pretence of being a child (suggested not only by the dress but by the girlish pose of the model) when clearly the model is not, is sexually provocative, provocative because of the confusion that allows the viewer to desire the child and the adult at once, or maybe, more accurately, to desire the ambiguity, to desire the suggestion of a transgressively incomplete sexual socialization.

But this is not, as some may object, simply the naughtiness of woman-child eroticism. In ads such as those for cK one, for instance, the transgression of the separateness between childhood and adulthood can be seen in young men as well. In one cK one advertisement, for instance, we see a young man who, leaning slightly back in a ready-to-provoke pose, casually exposes his stomach with one hand, while looking the viewer seductively in the eye. The casual exposure of the stomach suggests something a child would do; and yet, by the obvious maturity of the figure, the act takes on definite sexual overtones (the child's act may have similarly sexual overtones, but as such it would be, for the most part, considered relatively acceptable and even an "innocent" exploration of the body). The suggestion of simultaneously operative stages of sexual development, where no one stage is resolved and completed, once again suggests the refusal of the properly socialized body, one that would act appropriately to its designated stage in life, and would remain in that one stage. While this particular scenario is only visible in some of the ads I address in this essay, its implications—the refusal of assigned subject positions—are the same.

The refusal of category completion, the refusal to be properly gendered or sexualized into adult or child, or, more radically, as I suggested above, into man or woman, male or female, or heterosexual or homosexual, is a refusal of completion, of that completion that is essential to the normative social regime. In his essay on queer tactics and politics, Michael Warner calls these imperatives "regimes of the normal." Warner uses this phrase, "regimes of the normal," to underline the violence by which "normality" is enforced, stating, that "queer," by contrast, has the effect of pointing out a wide field of normalization, rather than simple intolerance, as the site of violence (Warner 1993: xxvi). Likewise, Eve Sedgwick suggests that "*queer* can among other things . . . refer to the open mesh of possibilities, gaps, overlaps, dissonances and resonances, lapses and excesses of meaning when the constituent elements of anyone's sexuality aren't made (or *can't* be made) to signify monolithically" (Sedgwick 1993: 8). Queer denotes the resistance to monolithic categorizations of identity, sexual or other. In this sense, the figures in these ads are queer figures; they show a raw, physical resistance to monolithic categorization of their identities. They blur the lines and boundaries not only of sex, sexuality, and gender but also of race, age, and propriety. The fidgety characters in any one of the cK one line-ups (Figure 2) form not a straight, but a *crooked* line, stand shamelessly in front of the camera, pierced and tattooed, in ragged, gender-bending clothes and various states of undress. They pout, pose narcissistically, and mix coy childishness with adult sexuality. One senses, in these images, a palpable, physical resistance to the finality of identity. Refusing this finality, this completion, is a refusal of the fullness (both literal and metaphorical) of the adult body. It is a refusal of what it takes to *get there*, that is, *nurturance*. Incompletion is in this way a form of hunger, an unfulfillment that can be seen as socially or politically productive (in refusing and thus resisting normative social identities), but also, as I have been suggesting throughout this article, as emotionally, psychically, physically exciting—a perpetuation of a status of having never quite arrived.

Black and White: Dramatizing Lack and Need

Let me turn now from the bodies of the models to the photographic methods used to craft these images of thinness, hunger, unfulfillment, and refusal. The photographers responsible for the advertisements of this study comprise a new generation of young photographers who favor a gritty, "realist," unprofessional-looking, documentary style of photography, most of which is shot in black-and-white.[7] Photographers such as Corrine Day, the first to photograph the young Kate Moss and the one often credited with bringing on this shift in fashion photography, as well as David Sims, Craig McDean, Ellen Von Unswerth, Juergen Teller, Wolfgang Tillmans, and Nick Night, to name a few, defined themselves and their art in opposition to the glossy, colorful fashion photograph of the 1980s. They opted instead for the gritty, stark, black-and-white style used by contemporary art photographers such as Larry Clark, Jim Goldberg, or Nan Goldin, all of whom photograph the urban margins. Many of these new young photographers got their start in the alternative presses of new "fringe" culture magazines such as *The Face* and *i-D* in Britain, style magazines that offered a high level of creative freedom and encouraged experimentalism. Like Clark, Goldberg, and Goldin, these photographers identified with the urban subcultures represented in the magazines and in their photographs. The larger fashion presses were themselves receptive to these photographic styles, and in fact the shift in photography toward a bared down, anti-frills, anti-glamor aesthetic corresponded to other changes in the fashion world, especially the new emphasis on streamlined minimalism in clothes and design. These shifts also corresponded well to the very creation of the designer diffusion line—secondary lines created by top designers to appeal to younger, urban-identified customers[8]—which necessarily rely on such cutting-edge, "of the moment" photographic styles for their advertising campaigns.

This new style of photography has been surrounded by a rhetoric of realism. In a 1993 interview, Corrine Day calls her photography "snapshot," "spontaneous" and "real" and says "I see my fashion as reportage. I don't think of it as fashion" (Pandiscio 1993: 88). Similarly, Juergen Teller, the photographer responsible for the hugely successful "Hugo" series, says of his subject, the model Werner Schreyer, "He is not standard pretty . . . He has dodgy sides and we have shot them, whereas other people won't or will retouch the images. I think it's because, in some ways, he looks like a normal guy so people can relate to him" (Compton 1996: 172). What is "normal"—i.e. real—about Schreyer are not only his physical imperfections, but his unpolished emotions and raw edges. As one fashion writer commented, Schreyer is "a crooked, bruised hero with a broken heart. . . and a self-assembly, not assembly-line, wardrobe" (Compton 1996: 171). His pained soul and mix-and-match wardrobe suggest that "the Hugo man" is one who is burdened by his experience in the world, but who, nonetheless, survives. He looks as if he needs some comforting but would not accept it. That he survives and simply goes on (in the sluggish, careless way I described at the beginning) is romantic, beautiful, real. What is real, then, are dejected, hurting subjects: dramatic figures who feel real precisely because they feel pain, because they seem to carry inside them a reservoir of intense experience and emotion.

Documentary photography has long focused on such figures. Dust-bowl migrants, sweatshop workers, panhandlers, street-dwellers, drug users and others whose life experiences have been filled with pain and hardship make up the history of this journalistic medium. In the history of documentary photography, as John Tagg tells us, the photographer, or the camera, positions the subject as lacking, as needing help, thus creating a drama of human experience—the experience of being in need—with which the viewer will identify and to which she or he will respond (Tagg 1993). These ads capitalize on the excitement of lack, withdrawal, hunger, or unwholesomeness by using the tools of documentary realism. Through the lens of the "reportage" photographer, through the lighting and the setting and the starkness of the realist style, the figures in these ads enact this drama not only of lack, as Tagg suggests, but of unavailability. The disaffected adolescents and young adults of the cK one ads (Figure 2) and the frail, thin, bare, unsmiling Kate Moss in the Obsession ad discussed above are derivative of the figures in the pictures of Walker Evans, Dorothea Lange, and Robert Frank, whose "candid" "snapshots" of abject bodies and miserable but noble souls were meant to unveil the "real" abject reality of the "regular" American. The contrived and dramatic performances of the real that we find in the work of these classic documentary photographers have been adopted by today's photographers in a move that is at once a direct adoption of this photographic language, and a conscious manipulation of its processes for inventing and staging the real.

The photographer, Susan Sontag has suggested, is like the *flâneur*, the bourgeois man of nineteenth-century France who, in his leisure, voyeuristically seeks out the city's dark, seamy corners and neglected populations. The *flâneur* and the photographer seek out the neglected realities behind the official ones (Sontag 1977: 55–6). The form those realities take is constituted through the camera lens, through the photographer's or *flâneur*'s eye, through the upper class's wish to identify with a romanticized vision of the life of the poor—a vision of a life experience that is truer and more basic, because of the pain of living that cannot be escaped. This pain and poverty is classically expressed in the documentary photograph through numbed and unsmiling faces—faces, the photographers seem to suggest, that speak for themselves, faces that speak simple, basic truths that must humble the (middle- or upper-class) viewer. The numbed and unsmiling faces in today's ads draw upon—and manipulate—these images and this tradition.

Today's ads engage in this discourse surrounding "the real," both drawing on its associations with lack and unfulfillment, and the extremity of experience that accompanies these conditions, and at the same time, selling a certain realist aesthetic at face value. These ads must be understood, in part, as belonging to a larger movement in one of today's dominant taste systems (middle- and upper-class), in which a look of unembellished realism and authenticity has come to represent a purer form of beauty. Creations of the real not just in black-and-white photography, but also in such items as the "rustic"-looking furniture of companies such as the Pottery Barn (even the name implies a realist rhetoric and a return to purer, "real-er" times) represent an unpretension in taste, crafted and displayed in material possessions that look old, simple, nostalgic, pure. The pared-down look of a chest of drawers (pared down to absolute simplicity—a divestiture similar to that of the body that desires and creates its own lack), painted to look old and even to seem as if the paint were peeling, denotes, like the black-and-white photograph of today, a return to truth. While the Pottery Barn does not have the "edge" that I refer to in realist photography, and this is an important distinction, it shares with the latter a larger system of aesthetics in which the real is constructed through divestiture.

Black-and-white photography seems especially suited to create such a realism in the stark and sharpened aesthetic it engenders through contrast and shadow. It lends itself well to the illustration of thinness, hunger, need, and unfulfillment. It heightens the sensation of lack, for to use black-and-white in an age when we have color photography is itself a rejection of fullness, of the filling happiness of color. To withhold color is to dwell *in* a lack, to emphasize starkness, angularity, and hardness over easy, happier softness. And to withhold color while photographing abject subjects, often in "trashy" settings, is, as I have suggested in this section, to evoke quite directly a photographic history entirely predicated on a drama of lack and need, in other words, of hunger. We don't want Kodachrome's nice bright colors, to paraphrase Paul Simon. We *want* everything to look worse in black-and-white.

Yet even as they employ all the standard tactics for photographing the real, we know that they are *not* photographing the real. Everyone *knows* these are models,[9] posing in advertisements, selling expensive new fashions. The manipulation of this knowledge in the advertisement is the final element we must consider to understand these ads.

First, we must keep in mind that in the realm of clever advertising today, where ads are created to capture the attention of a young, pop-culture-literate, advertising-literate, media-savvy MTV generation for whom the idea that advertising "brainwashes" is old news, no advertising image is produced with the intention of being read absolutely literally. Almost everything, in this realm of advertising, has a self-referential tone, a nod to the savvy viewer, or even a distinctly camp sensibility. In the case of the advertisements discussed in this article, consider just how well thin, abjected, depressed affects are enacted. That is, as we have seen, these figures are not simply burned out and numbed, they seem *determined* to show a lack of affect. They are not simply unsmiling, they are *resolutely* unsmiling. There is a deliberateness to their poses, an exaggeration to their unavailability, to their repudiation of the body as a site of warmth and nurturance. These figures are of course models, and therefore actors. By definition they are there to put on a look. That is part of the point. They are not just acting, they are letting us know that they are acting, and in this way seem to be saying: "we know that you know that we are performers." But what they are performing is the act of performance itself. By the very deliberateness of their posing and posturing, they seem to be suggesting these—the poses and postures, the *attitudes*—to be the very sites of articulation and formulation for the emotional and social subject positions that they are enacting. And of course, furthermore, these figures and images are *re*-enacting a realist language of photography and of pose that—as informed 1990s denizens of this culture and as inheritors not only of its traditions but of generations of critiques and discourses surrounding those traditions—we already know to be contrived. In these ways they are placing the emphasis on the performance and framing of the real. By focusing our attention on the posing and the posturing, the attitude, indeed the acting behind these abjected, withdrawn poses, by suggesting the staged and choreographed nature of these "realist" images, they show the real to *be* the pose and performance.

Conclusion

In this essay I have proposed a reading of a trend in fashion advertising today in which the models appear withdrawn, disaffected, and often unhealthful. I have suggested that the figures in these ads style themselves as unfulfilled and undernourished (in body and in soul) and that they do so in a deliberate and affected manner. There is a will to their hunger, to their thinness; a will to look bad, to look ethereal, pale, removed, unreachable. More than simply being empty, these figures *claim* an unavailability, an out-of-reachness. In this way they enact not a passive hunger but an active hungering.

Such poses, as I have noted, are not new, but have instead recurred in the figures and images of various avant-gardes and counter-cultures. These images draw upon this aesthetic style as it exists in our historical images, literature, and imagination, and as it exists today. I have endeavored to bring into view what I see as the passionate emotion behind this style, and the social messages and implications that these emotions might carry. In so doing I hope to have helped the skeptical viewer understand its appeal, and to share with the already friendly viewer my ruminations on just why we might like these ads so much.

Finally, I have proposed that part of what these ads *do* is show the representation of style to be as real as any other manifestation of style. What these images capture is the *act* of performance, the act of identity, of claiming and refusing emotional, social, cultural definition expressed through poses, postures, and affectations; in other words, through style. They, as images, and even more, as deliberately crafted images, show that if there is any "truth," it is in the style itself, and in what the style represents. I have examined pose and affect as pose and affect, and not as poses and affects bound to any bodies in particular. It is representation that concerns me, and the life of style—as social, emotional, political expression—in our visual imagination. If there are questions that I did not answer, or even ask, I hope that I have laid some groundwork for such further work. I hope, to be specific, that by seeking to explain *what* this detached, disaffected style and aesthetic expresses and means, I have done some of the work requisite to a study of *why* it has persisted historically, and has emerged with such force in fashion advertisements today.

Acknowledgements

I would like to thank Nancy Hewitt, Jan Radway, Bill Reddy, Noah Rosenblatt-Farrell, Nan Enstad, Julie Mell, Karmen MacKendrick and Patrick Wilkinson for their valuable comments and feedback on earlier versions of this article.

Notes

1. The commentary and controversies surrounding Moss's body occurred for the most part in the earlier years of her modeling. In the past few years, as she has matured in age, her body has changed significantly.
2. The standards for thinness have changed, but it is safe to say that in the twentieth century fashion models have always been relatively slender, and increasingly so over the course of the second half of the century.
3. For an exposition on the sublime experience of smoking, see Richard Klein, *Cigarettes Are Sublime* (Durham: Duke University Press, 1993).
4. For more on the nineteenth-century cult of invalidism and the "consumptive sublime," especially in how it relates to misogyny, see Bram Dijkstra, *Idols of Perversity: Fantasies of Feminine Evil in the Fin-de-Siècle* (New York and Oxford: Oxford University Press, 1986).
5. See Barnaby Conrad III, *Absinthe: History in a Bottle* (San Francisco: Chronicle Books, 1988).

6. This of course varies according to country and is probably most true of the United States.
7. When they're not in black-and-white, the color scheme of these photographs is often garish, putrid, or tacky, as, often, are the clothes, which, in their "campy" 1970s retro colors such as browns and rusts, dirty yellows and sickly greens, almost no one can wear and look healthy. Prada advertisements, for instance, have especially made use of such color schemes. The settings for these images are often equally tacky and "retro" 1970s. Such a tacky retro setting, the basement "rec room," was the setting for several of the Calvin Klein ads that were highly criticized and subsequently withdrawn a few years ago. They were criticized for being too sexually suggestive; but it was not just the insinuations of "underage" sexuality in these ads that upset people, but the seediness of the images. The seediness, along with the angle of the camera (the ads were criticized for being suggestive of a pornographic shoot), and of course the poses of the models, created an image or a performance piece (some were television ads) of gritty, unhappy, unclean "realism."
8. Examples of diffusion lines are: Calvin Klein's "cK," Versace's "Versus," Donna Karan's "DKNY," and Hugo Boss's "Hugo."
9. Whether they are glamorous professionals or people taken "off the street," as is sometimes the case these days, they are for all intents and purposes models, posing, even, as I have just argued, if posing "as themselves."

References

Berger, John. 1972. *Ways of Seeing*. London: British Broadcasting Corporation and Penguin Books Ltd.

Compton, Nick. 1996. "There's a New Boss Man in Town." *ARENA Homme Plus* Autumn/Winter 96/97: 168–72.

Conrad, Barnaby, IV. 1988. *Absinthe: History in a Bottle*. San Francisco: Chronicle Books.

Dijkstra, Bram. 1986. *Idols of Perversity. Fantasies of Feminine Evil in the Fin-de-Siècle*. New York and Oxford: Oxford University Press.

Ellmann, Maud. 1993. *The Hunger Artists: Starving, Writing, and Imprisonment*. Cambridge, Mass: Harvard University Press.

Hemingway, Ernest. 1990. "Hunger Was a Good Discipline." In *On Bohemia: The Code of the Self-Exiled*, ed. by Cesar Grana and Marigay Grana. New Brunswick and London: Transaction Publishers. (First published 1964.)

Klein, Richard. 1993. *Cigarettes Are Sublime*. Durham, NC: Duke University Press.

Kristeva, Julia. 1982. *Powers of Horror: An Essay on Abjection*. New York: Columbia University Press.

Pandiscio, Richard. 1993. "Corrine's New Day." *Interview*, January: 88–92.

Sedgwick, Eve Kosofsky. 1993. "Queer and Now." In E. K. Sedgwick, *Tendencies*. Durham, NC: Duke University Press.

Sontag, Susan. 1977. *On Photography*. New York: Anchor Books, Doubleday.

Tagg, John. 1993. *The Burden of Representation: Essays on Photographies and Histories*. Minneapolis: University of Minnesota Press. (First published 1988.)

Warner, Michael. 1993. Introduction. In M. Warner, *Fear of a Queer Planet*. Minneapolis: University of Minnesota Press.

Wright, Lee. 1992. "Outgrown Clothes for Grown-up People." In *Chic Thrills: A Fashion Reader*, ed. Juliet Ash and Elizabeth Wilson. Berkeley and Los Angeles: UCLA Press.

Yablonsky, Linda. 1997. "Wasted Beauty." *New York Times* (editorial), 27 May 1997, p. 15.

Fashion Theory, Volume 2, Issue 2, pp.151–164
Reprints available directly from the Publishers.
Photocopying permitted by licence only.

Dangerous Liaisons: Art, Fashion and Individualism

Robert Radford

Robert Radford teaches at Winchester School of Art, University of Southampton, UK. His research interests are purposefully eclectic, but have centered on problems of the relations between art and other ideological fields, including politics and fashion. His latest book is a monograph on Salvador Dali (London, Phaidon, 1997).

Throughout most of the recorded history of art, or rather of commentaries, evaluations and critiques of art, there has existed an almost unquestioned belief that an essential, almost a defining, feature of the nature of art is that it should demonstrate the quality of endurance. This is the justification for the museum. The statuary of ancient Greece was constructed in the most permanent materials available, and its physical survival into eras of Renaissance and neo-classical culture has further enshrined this evaluative idea. Another major idea developed alongside this concept of art's desirable state of longevity, and that was the idea of authenticity, which was equally related to the discourse of classicism, so that the two ideas became conflated. (Good) art survives because it in some way "contains truth," but art that has been neglected and forgotten has suffered that outcome justifiably, because it was of insufficient quality, it lacked truth, and did not "stand the test of time." Far from any relaxation of this idea during the period of Romanticism, this auratic concept of art and its powers of authenticity was augmented by a cult of art that directly equated art with truth. This situation continued to inform the ethos of the avant-garde within modernism, which, despite a generalized irritation with the inherited forms and with the social context of art, retained a hold on this dominant idea of authenticity, if anything elevating it even further, via the exhortations of Nietzsche, into the equation of art with spiritual and utopian truth apparent, for example, in the work and writing of Mondrian, Kandinsky or Malevich.

Fashion has, almost since its first recognition, been represented as art's "other." It has, until relatively recently, acquired no laudatory history, no museum of good example to pass down to future generations, no philosophy or critique; it has expanded within our culture without benefit of the academy. Whether from the position of Stoic, moral severity or Christian denunciation of sensuality, the preponderance of rhetorical commentary on fashion has, throughout history, been antagonistic. Fashion conflicts absolutely with these concepts of permanence, truth and authenticity, and is regarded as being particularly dangerous when it insidiously enters the citadels of art—Fiat modus pereat arus—as though virginal art were at constant risk of defilement.

It would seem, however, that all this system of values has recently shifted, now that the conditions of postmodernity and the demonstrations of the New Art History have exposed the insecurity of art's big ideas and have established a widespread cultural permission to recognize the new authenticity of fashion, in the sense that it most accurately reflects and communicates the values and complexities—the anthropological, if not the moral, truths—of contemporary, lived experience. Increasingly critics and curators are persuading us of the growing proximity between the practices of Art and of Fashion. Three major, recent exhibitions provide an adequate signal of this tendency; *Mode et Art* in Brussels and Montreal 1996, the *Biennale di Firenze: Il Tempo e La_Moda* in Florence in 1996, part of which was shown at the Guggenheim in SoHo, New York in 1997 and *Assuming Positions*, addressing "new crossovers in Fashion, Art and Pop" at London's ICA, 1997. It is alarmingly easy to designate this curatorial pairing as a fashionable position in itself. But further evidence of this tendency is widespread and is readily identifiable in specific statements and editorial strategies within influential art journals,[1] and furthermore there has been little attempt to refute its significance. I am as persuaded as most of these commentators that art has indeed been progressively taking on certain qualities most readily associated with fashion, specifically those three elements identified by Lipovetsky (1994) as seduction, ephemerality and discrimination within a genre.

I am less certain about the symmetry of the exchange, and doubt that an equivalent transition has emerged within the recent past out of fashion's relations with art. Certainly a cadre of designers have had their work exhibited in specific contexts that identify their products as art rather than designed commodities, and of course heterogeneous borrowings are constantly made from the visual field of art, though this only represents the continuity of a long-established practice, and it is notable that very little borrowing from that contemporary art that has been dominated by postmodernist strategies has seemed applicable (although it could be argued that a culture of irony and self-referentiality equally subsumes both practices). Fashion is still attentive to the residual aura attached to what is revealingly termed "high" art, however, and recent cases of using artists for modelling or engaging them to design the fashion show might be taken as instances of an attempt to procure the potency of this status by magical association.[2] The one area where the cultures of art and fashion appear to be most inextricably interfused, where common territory is most coherently shared, is that of the style magazine, aimed at a young market, where both the graphic presentation and the visual content and ideological position suggest a comfortable acceptance of shared values, linking dress, music, media and art. *Dazed and Confused*, published in London, can be taken as a current example of this tendency. Its imagery (for example, in the July 1997 issue) derives its punctuality precisely from the almost imperceptible distinctions between the visual representations on alternate pages of a cigarette advertisement and a graphic feature based on the work of an artist (Sarah Lucas) resembling a cigarette advertisement, or a fashion feature on knickers next to an article illustrating the erotic autophotography of Tokyo high-school girls. It represents a worldview familiarized, for instance, by the fashionable generation of young British artists, currently receiving international recognition, and it reinforces the insistence on the spectacular and the scopophiliac nature of today's generalized experience of viewing both art and fashion. Much of the power of engagement from this type of visual material derives, both for the creator and the user, from exercising the navigating skills required at the edges of category boundaries, from risking forays across borders of established genres, invoking a skilled aesthetic of fine distinctions.

The problem is, though, that there is a general danger here of category slippage, and there is a need to reach a little beyond the surface appeal of this pairing of art and fashion to clarify, through a set of categorical frameworks, the legitimacy, and even the logical validity, of such an identification of shared territory. The objective, even at the risk of a certain methodological crudity, is to reveal something of the cultural complexity that underpins the formation of the two fields, by distinguishing those elements that are properly held in common, at least to some extent, from those that are clearly discrete.

For these purposes the definition of "art" adopted is relatively straightforward: it is the field of production and usage defined by the institutions that train artists and that legitimate, promote, expose and create economic value for what artists make and do. "Fashion" is inescapably a more slippery term: for the most part it refers here to the conventional understanding of the field associated with the production and usage of clothing and personal appearance; but, on occasions, the use of the term "fashion" intentionally slips into a broader category of design and information that is definitively shaped by seduction and ephemerality. I am, throughout, conscious of the benefits of the theoretical model that Bourdieu (1979) develops in *Distinction*, where he argues for a separate consideration of the social, economic, and especially the cultural dynamics of the field governing production of a given commodity (in his example, *haute couture*) from the comparable factors that govern the field of the consumption of that commodity. I would want to adapt this model slightly in the light of de Certeau's argument in *The Practice of Everyday Life* (1984) that the term "consumption" implies too much of a docile passivity, whereas his preferred term, "user," reflects better the active, adaptive patterns of behavior characteristic of contemporary social being.

When the category "fashion" is expanded even further, in the thoroughly reasonable direction that Simmel,[3] for example, takes in his essay from 1904, when he requires it to include "Social forms, apparel, aesthetic judgements, the whole style of human expression" (1971: 299), it is obvious that, right at the outset, we are encountering different scales of comparative topography, in that, by this definition, the entire field of art would be subsumed within the territory of fashion.

Visual Culture

The most evident shared element is that of the phenomenological priority of the appearance and readability of information and semantic associations. Fashion's emphasis must be on immediacy of effect, on speed of communication. It has little expectation of second-level, more reticent or reflective aesthetic experience. It rejects emphatically any belief in a virtue of aesthetic durability, stimulating a positive distaste for a recently past style. Walter Benjamin, in his penetrating account of the meaning of fashion as a fundamental register of modernity under capitalism, developed in his notes for *Passagen-Werk*, frequently emphasized the crucial and instrumental aspect of repulsion from that which was judged to be outmoded, referring, for example, to "the fashions of the most recent past as the most thorough anti-aphrodisiac that can be imagined" (Buck-Morss 1990: 286).

Art has recently developed an emphasis on the immediacy of the surface, on the "one-liner" of an ironic statement, yet it still carries the burden of a tradition that expects second levels of visual or conceptual complexity and a period of valid usage extending beyond the immediate.

An indication of the residual auratic dimension attached to canonical works of modernist art and, at the same time, a recognition that systems of cultural evaluation were shifting, emerges from the literature that analyzes the case of the use by Cecil Beaton of a set of paintings by Jackson Pollock as the backdrop to a fashion shoot for *Vogue* in 1951. The critical reception of Pollock in the 1950s and 1960s was encoded largely in terms either of the existential suffering of the artist or of aesthetic formalism, and the ethic of either of these critical discourses would have been outraged by any suggestion of the fashionability of his art, let alone of its subservience to a fashion enterprise. The general critical reaction was that of psychological denial—it was never mentioned—until, significantly, 1990, with texts from Timothy J. Clark and Richard Martin, and later from Thomas Crow in 1996, which, relieved from the hegemonic pressures of the initial period and enabled by a critical worldview more skeptical of modernist idealism, were able to examine the issues raised by the event in more objective cultural terms.

Although elements of associated values—what might be called "poetics" of looking—enter the equation, the aesthetics of fashion design draw on the multidimensional complexities of form, color, texture and movement. The experience of its aesthetic qualities is enhanced for connoisseurs who are in possession of appropriate cultural capital, whether this be in the field of street style or fashion history. This need to be visually highly informed is a definite requirement of the fashion user, and this sophisticated ability to make small discriminations of judgment is acquired through the accumulated experience gained from shopping and surveying fashion magazines. In general, the aesthetics of fashion do not admit the spiritual, metaphysical or contemplative modes, although this territory is often approached in the work of certain Japanese designers or, at least, alluded to in fashion rhetoric, including the designer's own statements. There exists an area of significant ambiguity here; Issey Miyake specifically disclaims the role of the artist: "Fashion design is not art. I don't think it should be considered an art, or I an artist. I am not making clothes to have them displayed in a museum" (Tsurumoto 1983:103). Yet for the February 1982 issue of *Artforum*, a Miyake outfit appeared on the front cover; and he has of course featured as the fashion designer most regularly exhibited alongside conventionally recognized artworks in recent years.

The aesthetic values associated with art incorporate the sensual qualities of color, form and line, etc., but additionally invite the possibilities of conceptual deliberation or metaphysical contemplation. This makes certain demands on the connoisseur, such as the time for extended periods of encounter with the work and the possession of some specific cultural capital of art history or contemporary theory. However, the aesthetics of art and fashion would seem to have in common access to the poetics of associated ideas, allusions to place, history, erotics, rural or futuristic utopias, etc., all conducted in accents ranging between conviction and irony. The full range of treatment is also equally available to both fields, extending from the Apollonian values of balance, economy and restraint to the Dionysiac values of ornamentation, excess and waste.

Fashion provides a relatively unrestricted access for self-expression to the user through self-determination of body image; indeed, for members of certain social groupings, it often represents their exclusive arena for self-expression. From the point of view of the designer, too, there exists the perception of artistic self-expression in creating a collection; and there is sufficient ambiguity in the relations between couturier and client to support this, whereas the element of the designer's self-expression becomes increasingly restricted when designing for larger retail markets. In the field of art, expression is highly confined, by contrast, in that it is largely restricted to the contribution of the artist, despite the space conventionally appointed in current art discourses to allowing the viewer to complete the meaning of the art work, an approach which was classically developed by Eco in *The Open Work of Art* (1969).

Material Culture

Fashion shares with all design fields attachment to identifiable practical functions. Even the most apparently impractical virtuoso design must at the very least be wearable and must demonstrably allude to a potential lineage of sellable garments, as well as have the additional function of courting publicity. Fashionable practice is frequently a major element in communication and product design and in architecture, but there it remains constrained by specific material functions, whereas a reasonably effective definition of art is that it is a practice unburdened by extraneous function. All such terms as "applied art," "public art," "political art," etc., imply a qualification, a dissipation of the ideal of aesthetic disinterest that contributes to the aristocratic autonomy of high art.

Economic Function

Fashion is undoubtedly of vastly greater significance than art in terms of its economic importance, since, despite the fact that at one level it produces limited numbers of expensive, individual items in a manner somewhat comparable to art production, fashion's principal economic engagement is with industrial production, which has effects on a nation's trade and employment that have no equivalent in the field of art. This disproportionate economic power is interestingly not reflected in the relative cultural status of the two fields.

An individual work of art has a high unit price. This traditionally reflects the high unit cost of one-off production, but also acknowledges the influence of the art trade, which ensures that scarcity value and critical acclaim are directly reflected by price. Thus art can acquire an investment value and so function as a store of wealth. There is little equivalent to this trade in the field of fashion. The art trade is guarded and secretive about money, since there is the sense that it affronts the quasi-religious mystique inherent within art's traditions. By contrast, the fashion trade is blatant and celebratory about its cash nexus—after all, every item in the shop has its price ticket and the consumer is constantly engaged in making judgments on the basis of price.

The paradigmatic cycle of the fashion industry's seasonal rhythm of production is essentially economic in function, and all other design fields adhere to a logic of newness associated with a regular, temporal sequence, often punctuated by international trade shows. Whilst this seasonal logic is less axiomatic to the art world, it is not exempt from this effect; an artist wishing to maintain a successful career must expect to supply work for a sequence of dealers' shows and thematic group and personal retrospective exhibitions. There is also a hierarchical roster of art fairs and international biennials in which inclusion or exclusion has a direct effect on prices and reputation.

Sociological Function

The topic of fashion did not receive universal attention from the classic generation of the founders of sociology; but one figure, whose conceptual reach was notably wide-ranging, Georg Simmel, was particularly concerned with both fashion and the social experience of modernity. Simmel maintained that fashion served a primary social function as a means through which the contesting pressures of individual identity and social compliance are reconciled. This proposal still commands keen attention, especially if the term "fashion" is taken to embrace broader patterns of the dynamics of lifestyle and personal ideology, since it allows for the constant mobility of fashion change and the shifting dynamics of modern, complex societies.

Veblen's proposal, in the *Theory of the Leisure Classes* (1899), from much the same era, that fashion is a consequence of class competition and the constant need for a higher social class to discriminate its boundaries from the contending inferior class through the demonstration that it can afford waste, has survived less well and discloses its origins within the discourse of the moralistic critique of fashion, as well as being constrained by the limited development of fashion's place within society. It should be said, however, that Simmel fully shared Veblen's view that the social need for class discrimination provided the motive force behind the constant flux of fashion. However, the last hundred years have seen a revolutionary escalation of the operation of fashion within modern, Westernized societies, where consumer options and decisions are available at all economically active social levels. The fashion principle permeates all social life and is inescapable by any individual; all have to dress themselves and have to present themselves appropriately for their performance in society. This simple statement might be seen as sufficient in itself to satisfy this enquiry, since it is inevitable that the field of art production and usage is equally inextricable from fashion's societal pervasiveness.

The circulation and influence of art within the mechanisms of societal functions are much less significant. Historically, the association of art with the expression of aristocratic or state power has assured it a level of political significance, amply demonstrated in the case of the cultural history of France in the eighteenth and nineteenth centuries. But this power has largely ebbed away, and the social function of art rests in the area shared with other high-status leisure and lifestyle fields of provision. Despite modest levels of growth in access and popularity through publications and exhibitions, the social significance and circulation of art remains highly restricted and affords a very limited scope for social signification. Its social setting is comparable to the social groups that were traditionally served by *haute couture*, and even today the client bases for art and *couture* design remain closely congruent.

Fashion is therefore vastly more effective as a medium for social communication and signification, providing signals of class, generation, occupation, lifestyle and ideology; and these anthropological codifications can be extended to permit much more complex, subtle and usefully ambivalent readings in terms, for example, of gender positioning or "tribal" youth group identity, indeed in ways which reflect the complex and pluralist identities widely experienced today. Art would seem to have no comparable function of generalized social signification, outside its appeal to specialist publics; discriminations of taste in the production and use of art are essentially signalled only in terms of positioning along a continuum of ideological values between conservative and radical.

Of course this schematic comparison is necessarily rudimentary; but it might just serve as an antidote to the seductive allure of an unreflective pairing of art and fashion that too easily elides the two fields together and too blithely overlooks the differences of topography. Nevertheless, Lipovetsky's (1994) three defining characteristics of the fashion mode still survive the comparison, and we can chart a close congruency between art and fashion in terms of a shared dependency on Seduction and fantasy, Demand for the new, and Discrimination within a genre.

The first of these characteristics requires little expansion here, except to point out that it includes both the ostensible subject-matter and also the formal means of expression. It represents the appeal to the eye and to the senses, to the memory and to the imagination; it subverts objectivity, rationality and calculation.

The last of Lipovetsky's defining characteristics is potentially more contentious; but I would argue that highly comparable aesthetic judgments are operating when a shopper selects a preferred pair of trainers and when a curator selects the work of a particular artist working within a given genre of, say, narrative photo art or monochrome abstract painting. Certain aesthetic conditions cohere around a given genre that require designers or artists to vary, to explore and to interrogate the boundaries of that genre whilst simultaneously restraining them from so radical a move that the category and its criteria for evaluation are no longer recognizable. I have argued elsewhere (1994) that a contributory factor to the fashionable success of the work of Damien Hirst, for example, is the facility with which the viewer can place that work, visually, within the boundaries of established types, whilst at the same time recognizing sufficient elements of something newly added.

There would be much less room for disagreement about the third common characteristic of fashion and art, the compulsive attraction to the new. Under the reign of modernism in art, design and architecture, this compulsion was tied to the project of modernity and under the sway of the idea of progress: "newness" in art was expected and described in terms of "developments" and "experiment" according to an evolutionist paradigm that drew a direct analogy with scientific and technical innovation; as recently as 1976, Gablik's *Progress in Art* was still able to affirm this paradigm. This was the mode recognizable as avant-gardism.

Fashion, of course, during this same period, paid only occasional court to this one-directional idea of progress—simplification of cut, elimination of decorative detail, exploitation of new materials would be selected as concepts from time to time; but they would in due course be readily countered by contrary tendencies. This is not to deny the operation of some more graduated movements working at a deeper level of design morphology, responding both to changes in technical aspects of production and to the nature of lived experience, which must be accounted for in order to explain the fundamental transition in human appearance over the last century—but this is not the result of the operation of the fashion mode.

With the passing of the modernist ethos, art's previous "historically necessary" compulsion to the new has been replaced by a motivation indistinguishable from that governing decisions taken by designers working in any other fashion-led area. The culture of contemporary art, urged on by the dynamics of the art press, by gallerists and by artists' own ambitions and competitiveness, requires newness, but no longer expects nor believes in innovation as progress. This situation is, at one level, newly liberating; excursions can be made in all directions, history can be revisited, disrespectful appropriations are effected from the history of art, nomadic browsings can be made in exotic cultures and knowing borrowings made from the media of popular culture, including the culture of fashion—notably in the work of Silvie Fleury, Karen Kilmnik, Chris Moore and Beverley Semmes, amongst several others. Yet the cost of such relaxation from the rules of the paradigm of the avant-garde is heavy: it represents a trading down from "authenticity" to frivolity, and threatens to bankrupt art of its long-hoarded asset of the status attached to its cultural weight of seriousness. This leads to a fourth characteristic that should be added to Lipovetsky's list, and one that reflects the deepening hold of postmodernity: that is, the element of irony. Irony and self-reference pervade equally the high-profile currency of fashion design and advertising design, and even that of the more durable projects of architecture and product design, as well as contemporary art. They reflect a knowingness, a self-awareness, a lack of innocence, an impatience with the serious and authentic and an embrace of the frivolous that the artist and designer share complicitly with their audiences. The work of the group FAT—Fashion, Architecture, Taste—represents the current effects of the seductions of electronic, graphic imaging and the page spreads of the glossy architectural journal. An editorial comment in *AD* (July/August, 1996: 72), states: "Clearly the inclusion of the word 'Fashion' in the group's title hints at a territory that architecture might occupy—a volatile, fast moving, image-led territory, prone to quotation and parody, and lying outside the ghostly cloud that hovers permanently over that architectural project—the search for the authentic."

A promising arena for pursuing an historical understanding of the ever-growing permeation of cultural formations by the fashion mode lies within the discourse of individualism. Simmel shared with Baudelaire before him, and Benjamin after, the social anxiety compounded by the new experiences of metropolitan living. With the newly found promiscuity of social classes in the big cities, with the replacement of the former values of aristocratic privilege and refinement of taste by new values derived from the forces of capitalistic competition on the one hand and popular democratization on the other, Simmel perceived a general crisis in terms of assuring a sense of individual identity at the same time as maintaining social coherence. Fashion was therefore a necessary social mechanism to bring about this reconciliation: "Two social tendencies are essential to the establishment of fashion, namely the need of union on the one hand, and the need for isolation on the other" (1971 [1904]:301). Writing in 1987, Lipovetsky euphorically celebrates the culmination of the advance of individualization and affirms the fashion process as actively instrumental in its realization:

> By institutionalizing the ephemeral, by diversifying the range of objects, the consummate stage of fashion has multiplied opportunities for personal choice. It has forced individuals to inform themselves, to embrace novelty, to assert subjective preferences . . .

> under the reign of fashion we as individuals function increasingly as subjects of our own private existence; we are free operators of our own lives, owing to the surfeit of choices in which we are immersed. (1994 [1987]: 148]).

Maffesoli (1988), also writing in the nineteen-eighties, sees the process of individualization rather differently, however. He would agree with Lipovetsky in wanting to abandon the concept of class stratification and class competition that dominated nineteenth-century (what one might call modernist) sociological thought, but would claim that the process had in fact advanced further, that the inherent function of the individual had now become saturated, and that society was currently experiencing a phase of deindividuation. He proposes instead the concept of the "affectual tribe" to refer to the micro-groups that characterize contemporary [postmodern] experience, which is no longer shaped by the patterns of physical contact in metropolitan cities but by new affective networks facilitated by modern communications—E-mail, sexual contact lines, music festivals, support for football teams, etc.—which are maintained by the enabling power (*puissance*) of communal sociability and operate as a counter-force to the repressive power (*pouvoir*) of rationalist state politics. When Maffesoli looks at popular fashion, he sees, not the subtle token of self-identity within a permitted band of group normality that others might notice, but an affirmation of tribal identity: "The conformism of youth, the passion for likeness within groups or 'tribes', the phenomena of fashion, standardized culture, up to and including the unisexualization of appearance, permit us to claim that what we are witnessing is the loss of the idea of the individual in favor of a much less distinct mass" (1988 [1996: 64]).

Maffesoli's affinity groups cohere through shared aesthetics—through shared feeling—rather than through necessities of class identity or ideological rationality: their medium of cohesion is through style. Perhaps the apparent incursion of the fashion mode into the field of art that has been discussed above reflects the positions of its participants, both artists and users alike, who share these same conditions of loose and shifting affinity, guided in allegiance through style and fantasy and defended from the rationality of systems of dominant power by recourse to irony and frivolity.

De Certeau, in *The Politics of Everyday Life*, is in general less sanguine about the emancipatory effects of consumerism than either Lipovetsky or Maffesoli. His view is that as, progressively, the majority of people living in modern Westernized states are being excluded from the most significant areas of cultural production, in comparison with pre-modern experience, then that majority is becoming increasingly marginalized. The ruses by which those who find themselves culturally and economically excluded survive, are the tactics of "bricolage," of the subversion of received culture and of irony: "the tactics of consumption, the ingenious ways in which the weak make use of the strong, thus lend a political dimension to everyday practice" (1984: xvii). Irony is developed as a means of resistance, alongside the ruses, jokes and verbal trickery of popular speech and urban folklore, so as to withstand and subvert the more powerful forces of cultural dominance, rather in the manner of the effective cultural survival of the indigenous Americans under the Conquistadors.

What emerges from any review of the discourse of individualism is that the term can mean very different things at different periods and for different writers and, therefore, conclusions about the socially beneficial, detrimental or neutral effects of the (arguably) ever-increasing reality of this social condition are equally disputed. As Simmel reminds us, the original celebrants of the idea of individualism, figures like Rousseau, Fichte and Kant, nourished by the era of Revolution, conceived it as the means towards achieving the perfectibility of humanity, holding that every individual, reviewing his or her circumstances in the light of unfettered reason, would arrive at identical conclusions and (paradoxically to our later understanding of the concept) end up thinking and feeling about the world without difference from each other. There would be no place for fashion or any other frivolous cause for change in this worldview. Lipovetsky, reflecting contemporary existence, has argued that the trajectory of fashion directly parallels that of the rise of individualism within society and, moreover, justifies the logic of fantasy, playfulness and aesthetic discrimination, which unstoppably propels fashion onward today as a significant and instrumental riposte and antidote to the enormities of war and oppression that marked former eras of ideological absolutes. A more critical reading from these same conditions is plaintively summarized by de Certeau, "There are now too many things to believe in and not enough credibility to go round" (1984: 179).

As to the current relationship between fashion and art, let us admit the obvious, that it is not a relationship of equal partners. Fashion sweeps imperiously on, conquering, infiltrating and colonizing all areas of social, cultural and (lest we forget) academic enterprise. Inevitably art is subsumed within these processes; but what it retains to maintain its distance and its purpose is its resources of irony and nimble skepticism, with which, in the manner of de Certeau's tactics of the weak to subvert the strong, it can maintain an effective resistance.

Notes

1. The journals—*Frieze* in terms of its layout, *Flash Art* in terms of its editorial selection—must be noticed, but especially *Artforum*, which has in recent years included fashion commentary and set up "artist's pages" based on collaborations between artist/photographers and

fashion designers, such as Nan Goldin and Matsuda (Nov. 1996) and Juergen Teller and Vivienne Westwood (Feb. 1997).

2. Notably Haim Steinbach's design for the Strenesse Group, Milan, Spring/Summer collection, 1995.
3. Simmel addressed the significance of fashion in three essays, "Zur Psychologie der Mode," 1895, "Fashion," 1904, (published in German as "Philosophie der Mode," 1905) and "Die Mode," 1911. A valuable discussion of certain aspects of his theory of fashion is to be found in Jukka Gronow, "Taste and Fashion: The Social Function of Fashion and Style," *Acta Sociologica* 1993, 89–100.

References

Bourdieu, Pierre. 1979. *La Distinction: Critique sociale du jugement.* Paris: Minuit. Trans. by Richard Nice as *Distinction: A Social Critique of the Judgement of Taste,* London, Routledge & Kegan Paul, 1984.

Buck-Morss, Susan. 1990. *The Dialectics of Seeing.* Cambridge, Mass.: MIT.

Clark, Timothy J. 1990. "Jackson Pollock's Abstraction". In *Reconstructing Modernism,* ed. Serge Guilbaut. Cambridge, Mass: MIT.

Crow, Thomas. 1996. *Modern Art in Common Culture.* New Haven: Yale University Press.

de Certeau, Michel. 1984. *Arts de faire.* Trans. as *The Practice of Everyday Life.* Berkeley: University of California Press.

Eco, Umberto. 1969. *Opera Aperta*, Milan. Trans. as *The Open Work of Art*, London: Radius, 1989.

Gablik, Suzi. 1976. *Progress in Art.* London: Thames & Hudson.

Lipovetsky, Gilles 1994 [1987]. *L'empire de l'éphémère: La mode et son destin dans les sociétés modernes*, Paris. Trans. Catherine Porter as *The Empire of Fashion: Dressing Modern Democracy*, Princeton: Princeton University Press, 1994.

Maffesoli, Michel. 1988. *Les Temps des Tribus*, Paris. Trans. as *The Time of Tribes: The Decline of Individualism in the West*, London: Sage, 1996.

Martin, Richard. 1990. "Drip and Dress: a Metaphor of the Modern." *Textile and Text* 1990: 46–51.

Radford, Robert. 1994. "Art and Fashion, a Love Affair or a Shoot Out." *Issues in Art, Architecture and Design* Vol. 3 No. 2: 82–94.

Simmel, Georg 1971 (1904). *Selected Writings* ed. by Donald N. Levine. Chicago: University of Chicago Press, 1971.

Tsurumoto, Shozo. 1983. *Issey Miyake Bodyworks.* Tokyo: Shogakukan.

Veblen, Thorstein. 1899. *The Theory of the Leisure Class.* New York: Macmillan.

Fashion Theory, Volume 2, Issue 2, pp.165–192
Reprints available directly from the Publishers.

Breaking Habits: Fashion and Identity of Women Religious

Susan Michelman

Susan Michelman is an Assistant Professor in Consumer Studies at the University of Massachusetts-Amherst. Her research and publications focus on dress, identity and social change. Her Ph.D. in 1992 from the University of Minnesota and associated publications analyze cultural symbolism of dress in women's societies of the Kalaban people of Nigeria.

Nuns, or as those in non-cloistered orders prefer to be called *women religious,* are a striking case study for examining the symbolic relationship between fashion and social and personal identity. During the 1960s and 1970s, the majority of women in non-cloistered orders of the Roman Catholic Church, as part of larger reforms dictated by Vatican II in 1962, relinquished religious habits for secular fashions. Many had worn habits for a large portion of their lives, often between 20 and 35 years, dressing in them from the moment they arose in the morning until they retired in the evening. Their social identities were more outwardly visible than their personal identities, as they had relinquished individuality for a symbol of conformity in the eyes of the

Church. From the time that women religious first wore religious attire as novices, they were instructed to view themselves not as individuals, but as representatives of a group. Their habits symbolized their commitment and vows to the Church, which superseded their individual identities (Griffin, 1975).

I will discuss, from the perspective of symbolic interaction theory, how dress has played a critical and visible role in reflecting and helping to construct social and personal identities of women religious. Through the analysis of 26 open-ended interviews, I will discuss women's sequential dress changes from habit, to modified habit, and finally to secular fashion. These transitions have followed a historical progression, from the period prior to Vatican II to the present day. Likewise, the identity work that accompanied these transitions is linked symbolically to their changes in dress. I will analyze why the habit symbolized the precedence of social over personal identity, the modified habit identity ambivalence, and secular fashions the communication of their personal identity. The three photographs are visual documentation of one 84-year-old woman in the study, who was in full habit for over 30 years, and of her transition from habit to secular dress. All quotations contained within the article are anonymous, to maintain the confidentiality of the informants.

Ebaugh (1977), in her research on religious orders, confirmed that personal identity issues were not addressed by the Church prior to Vatican II. She describes the indoctrination of women religious as demanding ideological totalism (Lifton 1961). In her research, she discussed the mechanisms of social control that made totalism work. The symbolic gesture of exchanging secular dress for black religious garb was "the first symbolic gesture of 'putting off the world' and entering into a new life" (Ebaugh 1977: 21).

> The uniform was characterized by complete simplicity and modesty, being high-necked, long-sleeved, and ankle length. In addition to the uniform, feminine lingerie was exchanged for simple white cotton underwear, indicating that the postulant was exchanging her womanly enjoyments for austere dress that would now symbolize her as the spouse of Jesus Christ. In addition, henceforth the woman was no longer to be distinguished by dress from the other women in the institute with whom she would live (Ebaugh 1977: 21–2).

In contrast, the women religious in my study dressed in contemporary fashions that make them indiscernible from any other modestly dressed professional woman in American society. Some orders like their members to wear some visible indication of their affiliation as women religious, such as a ring or cross (Ebaugh 1993); but many of the women in my study did not. In this article, I will discuss how the habit, for many women in non-cloistered religious orders, came to be viewed by them prior to Vatican II more in a negative than a positive light. Their perception was that dress inhibited their ability to have positive social interactions as people; rather, they were frequently stereotyped by the symbolic nature of the habit. The habit visually symbolized and promoted interactions with others that reinforced this belief.

Currently, the work and lifestyles of women religious in active orders are highly liberated in contrast to what they were in the period prior to Vatican II. Women exhibit a high degree of personal autonomy, many living alone or in small groups fully integrated into the non-celibate lay community instead of in orders (Ebaugh 1993). Dress, seen in the light of the many social changes affecting women religious, has been critical not only in reflecting, but also in helping to construct social change for women religious, specifically through its role in symbolic interaction processes related to the formation and perpetuation of personal identity.

Theoretical Issues

Symbolic interaction (SI) theory asserts "that the self is established, maintained, and altered in and through communication" (Stone 1962: 216). Stone widened the perspective of symbolic interaction studies to include appearance as a dimension of communication, usually as a precursor to verbal transactions. Furthermore, Stone asserted that appearance is a critical factor in the "formulation of the conception of self" (Stone 1962: 216). Appearance establishes identity by indicating to others what the individual projects as his or her "program" (one's social roles of gender, age, occupation). In turn, these are "reviewed" by others, thereby validating or challenging the self (Stone 1962: 222).

> It [identity] is not a substitute word for "self." Instead, when one has identity, he is situated—that is, cast in the shape of a social object—by the acknowledgment of his participation or membership in social relations. One's identity is established when others place him as a social object by assigning him the same words of identity that he appropriates for himself or announces. It is in the coincidence of placements and announcements that identity becomes a meaning of the self and often such placements and announcements are aroused by apparent symbols such as uniforms. The policeman's uniform, for example, is an announcement of his identity as policeman and validated by other's placements of him as policeman (Stone 1962: 223).

Stone describes identity as being established by two processes, apposition and opposition, a bringing together and setting apart. "To situate the person as a social object is to bring him together with other objects so situated, and, at the same time to set him apart from still other objects." Identity, to Stone, is intrinsically associated with all the joinings and departures of social life. "To have an identity is to join with some and depart from others, to enter and leave social relations at once" (Stone, 1962: 223).

Goffman defines personal identity as "the assumption that the individual can be differentiated from all others" (Goffman 1963: 57). From an interactionist perspective, this was a real dilemma for some women religious in habit. Their dress clearly symbolized their total affiliation to their work in the order, but was described by them as "restricting" in their ability to interact and communicate freely. The consequences of these symbolic limitations were described by the women as causing them to "feel less than fully human."

Snow and Anderson (1987), in their research on identity work of the homeless, noted that while distinctions are made between identity and self-concept, the difference between personal and social identity is less frequently addressed. They define social identity as the attributes "imputed to others in an attempt to place or situate them as social objects." In contrast, personal identity refers to "self-designations and self-attributions brought into play or asserted during the course of interaction" (Snow and Anderson 1987: 1347). This definition of social and personal identity is relevant to my study, as I am examining how dress can symbolize both components of identity.

A symbolic interaction perspective emphasizes social process and meaning(s) and is relevant for explaining how and why these women negotiated their visual and verbal awareness of their appearance (Kaiser, Nagasawa and Hutton 1995). When the women emerged as visible females from the self-described "androgyny"[1] of how they felt in the habit, identity conflicts surfaced. Davis (1992: 25) described how dress serves as "a kind of visual metaphor for identity . . . registering the culturally anchored ambivalences that resonate with and among identities." Ambivalence is acknowledged by Davis (ibid.) to be natural and integral to human experience, and can be exhibited in symbolic issues of appearance.

The modified habit, worn by many of the women in this study for a brief period after Vatican II, is symbolic of the transitional phase between habit and secular dress, and a metaphor for the identity ambivalence that they experienced. Currently, full habits and modified habits are worn in some women's religious orders, although not by the women interviewed in this study. It is now more common to find women wearing habits in cloistered orders. Kaiser, Nagasawa, and Hutton (1995: 175) expand on Davis's (1992) discussion of ambivalence as it relates to appearance: "By definition, ambivalence entails being pulled in conflicting directions, or experiencing contradictory yearnings or emotions. Drawing on the notion of ambivalence, Davis focuses on basic polarities in identities (for example, masculine versus feminine, old versus young) that lead to a state of tension. In the case of women religious, ambivalence was manifested due to conflicts between their social identity symbolized by the habit and vow of poverty and their personal identity as they emerged into secular dress.

Davis (1992) is broadly interested in dress and its symbolic relationship to identity; but more specifically, he discusses his theories within the framework of fashion. Davis defines fashion by distinguishing it from style, custom, conventional or acceptable dress, or prevalent modes by stressing the importance of the element of change (1992: 14). While the term "dress" communicates elements of stability, use of the term "fashion" implies the added element of social change (Roach-Higgins and Eicher 1993). Roach-Higgins and Eicher (1993) state that religious dress resists fashion change and is automatically excluded from a study of fashion. My study of the dress and identity of women religious raises interesting questions regarding why women religious currently find it acceptable to acknowledge "fashion" as a component of their appearance while remaining committed to their vow of poverty, in all cases taken while they were in habit. I will discuss why, before Vatican II, the habit symbolized a material component of their spiritual vow of poverty.

Davis (1992), Kaiser, Nagasawa, and Hutton (1995), and Nagasawa, Kaiser, and Hutton (1996) examine the concept of ambivalence as it relates to issues of identity and fashion. As women religious moved from the social control of the habit to secular fashion, each decision they made about apparel became a fashion choice and was so viewed by others. For example, it was a struggle to decide where to buy clothes and how much to spend in view of their vow of poverty. Style choices were confusing, as was indicated by their reverting to fashions of the period in which they entered the order. Gender and sexuality, obscured by wearing the habit, became evident when the women came forth as visible females. I will argue that their ambivalence around these identity issues became expressed symbolically in their dress.

Identity issues for women religious must be situated in relation to their status and role within the Church. Status is defined as a named position within a group, and comes with certain rights, obligations, behaviors, and duties that are defined as roles (Turner 1968). Kaiser asserts that being cast in a role is facilitated by looking the part and dressing in a way that others have come to expect of a person in that role (1990: 193). The religious habit was an instant visual identification of the women's role or social identity. What was described as totally lacking prior to Vatican II by most women in the study was the expression of the personal, more human self.

According to Kaiser, role theory is rooted in the symbolic interactionist perspective (ibid.). Identity, or who one is, is closely related to role, or what one does. A person may internalize a number of roles, yet will use only a subset of these roles for defining the self (Hoelter 1985). Role is associated with structural requirements for a fairly routine or automatic performance, while an identity is more of a self-definition, and is of a more abstract and personal nature (Kaiser 1990). The appearance change for women religious reflects changes in role and identity. Although social roles were frequently discussed by the women during the interviews, what surfaced more consistently in the research were personal factors that entered into their decision to change from habit to secular dress. Identity issues clearly emerged from the set of interviews as a priority over role changes. One respondent noted:

> I guess you could compare it [woman religious] to other roles. How much of that role is integrated with your personality? It is a good thing the more integrated it is. On the other hand, if you *become* your role, then you can't function without the habit. Like a married woman, if her role has been mother or wife and that is the only role that they can put on, and then when the children are gone, what happens to her?

Using role theory, Bush and London (1960) discussed the disappearance of knickers* for young men, which reflected changes in their social roles in contemporary American society. They expanded their hypothesis to assert that changes in enduring modes of dress (for example, habits) are indicative of changes in social roles within a given society. Their conclusions regarding dress and social role might appear quite similar to the changes symbolized by dress for the women religious in my study. I would argue that the motivation for the women to change their dress was first and foremost an identity issue and secondarily one that reflected changing social roles within the Church. Life history information, ascertained during interviews, bears out the personal nature of their relationship to dress.

> I entered in 1948 when I was 23 years old. I am now 69. I was in full habit—everything—black serge and all the paraphernalia that went with that. Some of the people [women religious] talk about all the very difficult experiences they went through in adapting to religious life and so forth in our novitiate, training years. One of the hardest things for me was the habit. It was attractive, I really felt that it was; but it was not a comfortable thing to wear. I was a graduate nurse working as a nursing supervisor when I entered. A lot of the things I experienced I just thought, well, that is what you had to do to be a Sister. But in the back of my head, [I felt] those things were going to change someday. They weren't the essence of what religious life was all about.

* Knickers were knee length trousers worn in America in the late 19th and early 20th century by little boys. Their popularity diminished in the 1930s.

Some of the women who participated in the study have experienced role change within the Church commencing with Vatican II and their shift in attire. Other women's roles remained primarily unchanged. For example, one woman interviewed has a Ph.D. in social policy and is currently the president of a hospital system. Although she is clearly an accomplished woman in her own right, as a religious within the Church she exemplifies the potential for non-traditional roles. In contrast, another woman interviewed gave up her full habit only reluctantly several years ago after wearing it for 34 years. A hip injury made it difficult to dress herself. Her contention was that the habit was "irrelevant" to her work in the community and her self-identity, which had never changed in interest or direction.

> The interesting thing was that with the habit I felt that I was accepted wherever I went. I found that once people got to know me, that the habit was part of me, but it wasn't [all of] me. I was at Springfield at that nursing program in full habit which meant that I went to all the secular hospitals. I thought hopefully, I always look beyond the people's dress to what the person is and I would hope that they were doing the same with me. With that philosophy, I went through 17 years with all the students and had absolutely no problem.

In my study there was no common consensus about roles for women religious. Some women would like the ability to become a priest, while others want roles to remain consistently the same. Nonetheless, the overriding power of the Church remains the Pope, who has resisted a more liberal approach to the roles of women religious, particularly with regard to their becoming priests. The women's potential for changing identity is more within their personal grasp than their ability to change roles within the patriarchal confines of the Church.

Research Method

The twenty-six women who participated in this study are members of non-cloistered orders in western Massachusetts, USA, who adopted secular dress in the 1960s and 1970s. Other orders that were in the forefront of changing dress started as early as the late 1950s.

One-hour, open-ended, transcribed interviews on their experience of exchanging religious habit for secular dress have allowed me to examine the social and psychological implications of this event from a personal perspective rather than examining this issue as a strictly social phenomenon. I chose the interview process as my primary methodology because I wanted each woman's voice to be clearly expressed. Interviewing is an effective method to gain access to people's thoughts, ideas, and memories in their own words rather than those of the researcher. Some feminist researchers propose that women interviewing other women is a particularly effective method as a result of the common understandings in woman-to-woman talk (Reinharz 1992).

My research follows an inductive, grounded theory approach, originally proposed by Glaser and Strauss (1967) and later examined as an effective method for textiles and clothing research by Boynton-Arthur (1993b). In compliance with this process, I entered the project without a working hypothesis and relied on interview data from the women to direct the research, which was serendipitous (Glaser and Strauss 1967). More specifically, my interest in a symbolic interaction explanatory framework emerged from examining the data. In accordance with Strauss (1987) I found that I needed to be fully aware of myself as an instrument for developing theory.

I interviewed each woman in her home or work environment, which I felt allowed her to open up concerning her personal experiences related to dress and identity. This was important because until the time of Vatican II personal expression, particularly in the area of dress, was extremely limited. The habit, indicating symbolic social control, reflected deeper issues of total devotion and obedience to the church. My research was facilitated by discussing the relinquishing of the habit 15 to 20 years after the event, allowing women to arrive at some degree of comfort with their identities and related appearances.

A significant aspect of this study is that outsiders, like myself, have not been readily welcomed by women religious to conduct research within their organizations. I began my study by discussing the research with presidents of two orders, who were also leaders within the community of women religious. I found that their recommendation of other women religious who might be available for interviews clearly opened many doors.

A one-to-one interview setting was conducive to observing non-verbal communication. For example, repeated postponements of a scheduled meeting, body language during the interview, and what was worn clearly had implications for interpretation. I have selected segments of interviews to illustrate my more conceptual or theoretical approaches to questions of identity work. To retain anonymity, interviewees will not be identified by name.

This particular method of research is labor-intensive. For each participant in the study, there is about 20 hours of my work involved, from ascertaining the subject and obtaining permission to do the interview to then following through with all aspects of the interview, as well as analyzing and processing the data. Each interview, when transcribed, is approximately 12–15 pages of typed data. The process of analyzing the data is based on my own prior experience doing ethnographic research on dress in Nigeria (Michelman 1992; Michelman 1995; Michelman and Eicher 1995). My method of analyzing the data consists of reading and searching for themes in the interviews in conjunction with my own notes and observations prior to, during, and after the interview. This includes any telephone calls, written communication, photographs shared by the women, non-transcribed interactions at the time of the interview, etc. The analysis process consists of noting consistencies and differences between interviews. For example, I examined how long it took for the women to leave full habit for modified habit and then for secular dress. I found there were certain common social and historical events that impacted on all the women. In contrast, each woman also had her own unique story to tell.

I have found unstructured open-ended interviews to be particularly effective for examining issues of dress, identity, and social change. The importance of the one-to-one relationship established between interviewer and interviewee is a critical component in uncovering the more personal and abstract issues of dress and identity. I have found this method particularly effective for gaining a deeper understanding of the relationship of identity to appearance. Although this is a highly labor-intensive form of research, the quality and depth of the data prove its worth.

Social Identity and Life in the Habit

Habits are a type of uniform that identifies group membership and helps ensure that organizational goals will be attained (Joseph and Alex 1972: 719). "The ambiguity ordinarily attached to the stranger in modern urban society is absent for the uniform-wearer, whose group membership, and perhaps his rank, seniority, and prior achievements, are proclaimed by his apparel" (Joseph and Alex 1972: 725). Uniforms reveal and conceal statuses, act as totemic emblems that embody the attributes of a group, suppress personal identity, and certify in a symbolic way the legitimacy of the group.

In contrast, for most people, dress is typically changed according to the needs of an individual's social interaction, even for those whose social roles are highly associated with their clothing. For example, police or military uniforms that identify the wearer within a work-related context can be relinquished in other settings. In Muslim cultures, veiled women usually remove that item of apparel in the presence of immediate family members. In contrast, women religious prior to Vatican II were always identified in habit, even within the context of private interactions with other Sisters (Figure 1). Religious orders were quite homogeneous both in exterior manifestations such as dress, and in the purpose and spirit that permeated them (Ebaugh 1977: 13). Their personal and social personas were one and the same. The life of a woman religious was highly prescribed and routinized. This point is succinctly described in one of my interviews regarding life in habit:

Interviewer: When was the time of day when you were out of habit? Was there a time when you could take this habit off and be more relaxed?

Respondent: You were in it from 20 minutes after five—later on ten minutes of six until 8.30 every night. Everything was done in unison. If we would have recreation at night which would be maybe 7–8, we all re-created in the same room. Recreation would consist of sewing. On special occasions we had movies. You were still always together. We always said "our" . . . "our" habit.

Enforced isolation from the outside world and rigorous resocialization characterized their lives. Resocialization refers to socialization into the life of the order, involving a radical departure from prior identity and experience to produce dramatic differences in self-image, beliefs and behavior. This process involved relinquishing the individuality of dress choice, deferring to the uniform appearance of the habit. At each stage before taking final vows, the woman was encouraged to give up her prior self-image, accompanied by a commitment to learn to conform to the demands of her new role as a woman religious. Postulancy was the first stage, at which she received a black uniform, was asked to give up her personal possessions, and was limited to infrequent contact with family and friends. The postulant's uniform varied slightly from order to order, but mainly consisted of a short white veil, a blouse and a black serge skirt. She was segregated with other postulants and together they began to learn the general expectations attached to becoming a Catholic woman religious.

If she successfully completed this initial period, the postulant proceeded to enter upon her novitiate, a year isolated from everyone except other novices. In a ceremonial rite of passage, novices received the habit, a religious name, and a new identity as bride of Christ. As is stated in the Ceremonial for the Reception of Novices of the Sisters of Providence, each component of the habit is symbolically linked to their vows. The habit symbolized an enduring state of humility; the cincture, a sign of chastity and temperance; the tunic, a sign of gravity and modesty; and the white veil, a sign of innocence (Ceremonial for the Reception of Novices, 1913). During the ceremony, the novices were given these individual symbols, and later returned robed in the complete religious habit.

Figure 1
Sister L. is photographed on the right in full habit of the Sisters of Providence in Massachusetts in the 1950s.

During the final period of her training, if she was accepted, she took vows of poverty, chastity, and obedience, and retained limited access to the outside world. In my interviews, I learned that heads were shaved prior to making final vows as a symbolic gesture related to the vow of chastity. Hair became both a public and private symbol for these women. As Obeyesekere (1981) argues in his essay on personal symbols and religious meaning, public symbolic behavior, such as cutting the hair, can have psychological meaning clearly linked to the identity of the individual. One of the women confirms this in the following quote. "When we had it done [had the head shaved], it was to connect to the vow of chastity. You were sacrificing a precious gift [hair] and after that it grew back in, but it was a symbol just before you made your vows."

If one were to seek to place these women religious in full habit on a dress continuum at one end of which appearance during most of the hours of the day is closely associated with a social identity, while at the other end is to be found the clothing non-conformist exhibiting a high degree of personal identity, then one would have to place them very much at the pole at which it is the social identity that is almost exclusively depicted. In such an extreme situation, the women had virtually no ability to display personal choice or individuality in dress.[2] These aspects of life, which most people take for granted, were strictly routinized. Most women I interviewed felt this was highly negative and was an impediment to social autonomy and the ability to blend in. The habit was a "walking cloister" (Neussendorfer 1964: 72). For example an interviewee spoke with some candor about her inability to remain anonymous when traveling:

> I was going to Florida to visit my folks and the social workers from the children's center asked me if I would pick up a baby [for adoption] while I was there. We made a stopover in Atlanta and here I have this little baby boy in my arms and this woman came up and accosted me about the fact that because these sisters take these babies, you are encouraging young women to have children out of wedlock. If only I had not been in the habit, nobody would know, you know. They wouldn't have said a thing.

The Modified Habit: Identity Ambivalence

In the 1950s, under the leadership of Pope Pius XII, the dialogue on habits between women religious and the hierarchy of the Church was expanded. In a speech to the First International Congress of Superiors General of Orders and Congregations of Women in 1952, the Pope stated:

> The religious habit should always express the consecration to Christ; that is expected and desired by all. In other respects the habit should be appropriate ["conform to modern demands" in another translation] and in keeping with the demands of hygiene. We could not refrain from expressing our satisfaction at the fact that during the course of the year a few congregations had already taken some practical steps in this matter. To sum up: in things that

> are not essential make the adaptations counseled by reason and well ordered charity.

In 1962, Pope John XXIII implemented Vatican Council II and mandated a challenge to religious orders to renew themselves through critical examination of and experimentation with alternative versions of the structures, roles, and relations that formed the core of religious life (Ebaugh 1993). The women religious, particularly those in active orders, took this very seriously. Changes included returning for more education, (some of the women interviewed have completed masters' and one a doctoral degree), moving away from a cloistered lifestyle, and expanding their social service work into more diverse aspects of the community, and in addition re-evaluating their relationship to the habit:

> The religious habit, an outward mark of consecration to God, should be simple and modest, poor and at the same time becoming. In addition it must meet the requirements of health and be suited to the circumstances of time and place and to the needs of the ministry involved. The habits of both men and women religious which do not conform to these norms must be changed (Decree for Renewal of Religious Life, NCWC translation, Number 17).

Women in my study discussed the transitional period after Vatican Council II with mixed emotion. They felt that it was both positive, from a development and growth perspective, and negative, because of the disorder and dissension created while they re-evaluated identity issues. Debate on the habit among the religious themselves appeared in Catholic journals (Elizabeth 1965; Lesousky 1967; Roberts 1967; Neussendorfer 1964; Tate 1967). In addition, surveys and studies done in the 1960s indicated ambivalence and even displeasure among the laity on the subject of religious women's move to secular attire (Carlan 1969; Baer and Mosele 1970).

According to a census, between 1960 and 1975 the number of Catholic nuns dropped in the United States from 168,500 to 131,000 (SanGiovanni 1978).[3] The habit became a symbol of their identity conflict.

> *Respondent:* I can remember discussions at our chapters that went on for hours about change in habit. When I look back on it! That is how important the habit was to people.
>
> *Interviewer:* Do you remember some of the debate pro and con?
>
> *Respondent:* Well, the younger we were, the more in favor we were of changing the habit, obviously. The decision we made was that it was possible to remain in your old habit if you chose to do so. It still is acceptable.

> Or, you could go into a modified habit. That was the first step.

Some of the significant changes that occurred during the 1960s and 1970s were a decentralization of authority within orders and a system that allowed personal financial accountability. In the early stages of changes after Vatican II (mid-1960s), women had asked permission to take clothing and personal items from a common closet stocked by the order (Ebaugh 1993: 70). The allowance was minimal at first ($25.00) but was soon increased to allow women more autonomy.

The habit retained an important presence in women's social identity during the transition to secular dress. This interview indicates the depth of some women's ambivalence regarding the symbolic nature of their appearance during this period:

> I was going to have a meeting with the Sisters to tell them that I was planning to become Director of Education starting in the summer of 1968. I was so afraid that if I got up in that auditorium in front of those 700 women on Monday in this new dress, they would not hear a word I said. I made a personal decision to go back into the habit for that one day. They needed to hear what I was going to say because the whole job that I wanted to do could be ruined if they were not really with me in what I wanted to do. So I went back into the habit for that one day. My case was to get them on the band wagon [of education]. But that was the end. Then I took the habit off. I guess that shows you how symbolic it really was.

The actual appearance of these modified habits varied widely from order to order (Figure 2):

> *Interviewer:* What was a modified habit?
> *Respondent:* At that time [1960s] a simple dress, either black or white. I guess now I would call it a uniform. At that time a number of companies came up with the design and you could get them through a catalog. In our community we had a number of women who were talented seamstresses. We made all ours.

Figure 2
Sister L., photographed in 1969, is shown in her modified religious habit. This is the same woman shown in Figure 1.

Plogsterth (1975) discussed some of the historical dimensions of this period of transitional dress, including the unlikely and somewhat unsuccessful participation by the fashion industry (Figure 3) in the re-design and modernization of habits for orders such as the Daughters of Charity of St Vincent de Paul (Christian Dior) and Society of Christ Our King (Hattie Carnegie) (Figure 4).

The modified habit was frequently discussed by women religious in terms of its role in the transition to secular dress and not of its inherent value as a permanent dress change. The following interview transcription from a woman who had returned to college to complete a master's degree illustrates this point: "In 1976 when I was at Boston College in a program of religious education, as part of the program we dressed more casually. We [were in modified habit] and decided not to wear the veil. Four of our sisters had taken the program at Boston College. They were the ones that felt that they were being distinguished from others by their garb. They didn't want to be singled out because of the habit." The archivist of one order participating in this study shared a ballot with me that was distributed to all members in 1966 by the Costume Committee:

> Questions regarding all aspects of attire were evaluated by the members. For example, in responding to the question "Would you prefer to retain a one-piece habit?," 369 answered yes and 34 no. "Would you like to have our pectoral cross made smaller?" was responded to with 140 answering yes and 251, no. They also voted their approbation of waist length veils as opposed to shorter (and seemingly more practical) shoulder length. These votes indicate that there was conflict and confusion among members themselves regarding the transition away from the traditional habit.

One of the orders in the study had a unique approach to the problem, as described in the segment of and interview quoted below:

> When we began, we used material from the habits and we made modified habits. They still had to be black and white when we made that decision. We had a huge gym and we set a night when we were going to have a fashion show. We invited everybody over there because there were some feelings—there were some that resisted it. We invited people to come and look and the people that had decided to change . . . we had a piano playing and we walked around the gym. We were pretty freaked out, I have to tell you. We had seen other communities where they were divided down the middle over habits. We did not want that to happen to us because of what we wore.

By the 1970s most orders in my study began eliminating not only the habit but also the modified habit as well. Their transition to fully secular dress allowed them full and visible emergence as indistinguishable members of lay society.

Figure 3
Proposed design for habit modernization by Federico Mario Schubert that appeared in *Life Magazine* December 15, 1952, Vol. 33, p. 16.

Personal Identity: Women Religious and Secular Fashion

During the period of emerging personal identity, the women experienced profound conflicts surrounding dress and its complex relationship with their vow of poverty. The essence of the vow of poverty of spirit is humility, which is facilitated by material poverty (Metz 1968). The habit had come to be accepted as a visible symbol of humility, while fashion and cultural issues of women's appearance, such as make-up and hair style, were historically associated with worldliness and materialism, i.e. fashion. Yet, women religious found themselves visibly re-entering the secular world from the perspective of appearance (Figure 5).

Because of their vow of poverty, there was little money for clothing. Most of their attire post-habit came as hand-me-downs or from thrift shops. Currently, style-conscious Americans regard second-hand clothing as not only economically and politically correct, but also fashionable. This was not the case in the 1960s. Women religious discussed feeling awkward at their inability to put together what they considered a proper appearance.

> Three of us were in Florida right after the renewal. We went to visit a friend in one of the big hotels and there were three very wealthy women sitting at the entrance of the dining room. When we walked by them, I heard one of them say, "They look like they just came out of the Salvation Army!" I laughed, but the other [Sister] did not have a sense of humor. We were told we could go into secular clothes but we had no money and nobody helped us.

The habit had obscured visible markers of womanhood such as the hair and figure. In my interviews, much discussion focused on the personal discomfort and even trauma of re-emerging into secular society. Skills related to personal appearance had to be re-learned. Hair was discussed frequently as the focus of anxiety. After years of deprivation of air and light under the habit, hair loss was common. In this interview segment, a woman religious discusses her personal viewpoint on hair:

Respondent: I saw older women buying wigs who had lost their hair because of the habit.

Interviewer: Was that because of rubbing?

Respondent: Yes, and also because they didn't get air. Even at night they wore caps.

Interviewer: Was this a permanent hair loss?

Respondent: Yes, for some. But for some it was O.K. [it grew back]. I color my hair. It's something I do for myself. In the 1960s we began to do a lot of more personalized and psychological study of ourselves. The

Figure 4
Proposed design for habit modernization by Mameli Barbara that appeared in *Life Magazine* December 15, 1952, Vol. 33, p. 16.

> spiritual was always part of it. How can you separate the spiritual and emotional? It's holistic.

The habit had given women religious surprising freedom from the tyranny of appearance experienced by women in North American culture. Women religious were confronted with issues of body weight that had previously been obscured under the folds of black serge. Some women interviewed went on diets. Their awareness of style and fashion became evident. Women made personal choices about make-up, jewelry, modesty issues (length of skirt, neckline) and even hair coloring.

Figure 5
Proposed design for habit modernization by Hattie Carnegie that appeared in *Life Magazine* December 15, 1952, Vol. 33, p. 16.

The move to secular dress had a dramatic impact on both women religious and society in general. "It revealed to the world in general the human being underneath the habit. But more important, it revealed the nun to herself: It was an experience in recognition" (Griffin 1975: 79).

> I entered in 1939, so I had been in the habit for 30 years when Vatican II came along and we began to make all the changes. The changes were much deeper than the habit. They were radical changes. While I had been in habit for 30 years, it was really no hassle for me to get out of that habit. It was real—it was absolute freedom. What it said for me was "I am no longer just a Sister of St Joseph. When I choose the clothes I want to wear, appropriate to me, I am Mary, who happens to be a woman who is a Sister of St Joseph."

Women in the study have discussed how secular dress and their re-emergence as visible females caused changes in their interactions with males, particularly those in the Church. Some women found their

Figure 6
Sister L. (on the far right) is shown in secular dress in the late 1970s with other members of the Sisters of Providence. This photograph is particularly interesting because it illustrates the diversity of dress and identitiy present in this order at this period of time.

relationship with men more problematic because they were no longer shielded by "the walking cloister" (Neussendorfer 1964: 72). In contrast, some women felt that relationships with males became more human.

Women emerged from habit during the turbulent period of the Civil Rights Movement, the Vietnam War, and the Women's Movement. Whether in habit or not, women religious are known for their involvement in social causes. Several women in the study referred to themselves as feminists, noting that historically they were role models for women who chose lives of dedication rather than marriage and family. Women religious also acknowledged their identities as single, professional women and their continuing conflicts with the patriarchal structure of the Vatican. They have been active participants in social activism and the dual labor market of the parish, where they have frequently, despite achieving higher education than priests, been denied positions of authority and participation in aspects of the liturgy.

Their emergence from habit to secular fashion not only reflected gender controversy within the Church but also helped women construct new identities as educated and professional women religious, rather than cloistered icons of the Church. Two women in my study referred to identities of women prior to Vatican II as "women of service" or, more derogatively, "handmaids of the Church." In a symbolic feminist action after Vatican II that coincided with the elimination of the habit, many women religious dropped the male component of their chosen names and reassumed the female.

> There was something else going on . . . we were changing our clothes and we were also changing our names. It didn't happen like Friday and Saturday, but it happened that we just kind of rebelled against having men's names—Sister Mary Peter, Sister Mary John, Sister Mary Bartholomew. Many women religious were moving out of their dress identity and they were changing their names back. All that was happening at the same time.

Discarding the habit was perceived by the women in this study as a positive step towards allowing them to work and interact as human beings while interpersonal distance lessened. In a positive sense, the Church, before Vatican II had viewed the habit as a protection against the evils of the world, yet that caused many religious to perceive themselves as isolated and inhibited from mingling with the people. Women religious in this study perceived secular dress as essential in allowing them normal, daily, human interactions, which greatly enhanced their ability to provide social service within the community.

> [People] tended to put women religious [in habit] on a pedestal. They didn't let us be human. They didn't recognize we are just like you—struggling with all the human things you struggle

> with . . . We are lay people just like you. I've chosen another way to live but it is not a holier way—it is a different way. There are many people out there who want us to go back into the habit because it speaks to them. I don't know what it speaks to them. I do know it makes a major difference in ministering with people. I knew it right away.

Conclusion and Implications of the Study

I have examined how the symbolic development from habit, to modified habit, and finally to secular fashion symbolized identity work for Roman Catholic women religious. Life in habit was characterized by ideological totalism, where the women, from dawn to dusk, were viewed by themselves and others as having a rigorously social identity. The habit, symbolic of the vows taken to become a woman religious, communicated the nature of their personhood. In the mid-1960s, after Vatican II mandated reforms, women religious entered a period of questioning prior institutions, including the habit. This was a particularly tumultuous period in the orders, as evidenced by declining numbers of entrants as well as an increase in defectors (Ebaugh 1977, 1993). The habit and the importance of its symbolism to the identity of women religious came under scrutiny, particularly from the women themselves. The current reflections on dress by women religious indicate the dynamic and ambivalent nature of appearance in its critical relationship to identity.

Some women who had been in habit for between 10 and 35 years were confronted with dress choices that challenged their frame of reference. For example it was a struggle to decide where to buy clothes and how much to spend in view of their vow of poverty. Style choices were confusing, and many women reverted to fashions of the period in which they entered the order. Gender and sexuality, obscured by wearing the habit, became evident when the women came forth as visible females.

I have used symbolic interaction theory to analyze how dress for women religious both reflected and helped construct identity. Identity ambivalence management is helpful in promoting an understanding of how the modified habit visually symbolized identity conflicts experienced by the women religious (Davis 1992; Kaiser, Nagasawa and Hutton 1995; Nagasawa, Kaiser, and Hutton 1996). The women's emergence into secular fashion indicates identity work that helped them make the transition from the habit to the ambivalence of the modified habit and their final acceptance of secular dress.

Davis (1992) addressed the concept of ambivalence and appearance more directly than other symbolic interactionists who preceded him. He argued that personal identity announcements and social identity placements might not be congruous. Many possibilities exist for incongruity (for example, a person might dress as a police officer for a costume party and be incorrectly identified as someone who is actually responsible for law enforcement). Davis (1992: 25), maintaining that dress serves as "a kind of visual metaphor for identity . . . registering the culturally anchored ambivalence that resonates with and among identities," suggests that personal and social identity incongruity occurs regularly because dress is often an ambivalent form of communication. Goffman (1959) makes the same kind of point in discussing "images given" and "images given off." My own research focuses on how a social identity, as conveyed by the religious habit, communicated an image that was incompatible with the personal identities of the women religious who wore habits.

I have examined the relationship between the meaning of the women's physical body, symbolized by their dress, and the social body of the Roman Catholic Church. This dialectic is a critical one in understanding the power of dress in both reflecting and constructing social change for women religious. For example, both Marx (1967) and Durkheim and Mauss (1963) argued for the dialectic between the "natural" and "social" body. Other social scientists have viewed the body as a *tabula rasa* for socialization. Van Gennep (1960), Mauss (1973), Bourdieu (1977), and Douglas (1966, 1970) have argued this dialectic to demonstrate the social construction of the body.

Comaroff's research (1985) on the Tshidi people of South Africa bears an interesting and instructive relationship to this study. Comaroff examined the manner in which symbolic "schemes" (for example, dress) mediate structure and practice. Through both historical research and anthropological fieldwork, she analyzed how the body mediates between self and society, specifically through her analysis of uniforms worn by both men and women in the post-missionary and post-colonial Zionist Church in South Africa. She discovered how these uniforms mediated a complex interdependence between domination and resistance, change and perpetuation. Likewise, she explored the meaning of liminality in such a context. Liminality is defined as an interstructural or transitional situation during rites of passage (VanGennep 1960; Turner 1967). In the case of the Tshidi, uniforms symbolized the transition they made from liminality, created by radical social and cultural change, to political resistance.

Comaroff explains how uniforms attained an important role in all South African Churches from the start by distinctively marking converts as those who were "civilized" by the missionary message. Whereas indigenous dress, i.e. precolonial appearances, clearly made visual the female and male reproductive body, the uniform of the Zionist Church covered not only the organs of reproduction, but obscured visual signs of femininity, masculinity and social status. Comaroff concluded that this appearance, through many signs that were comprehended by members of that society, was constructed of elements acknowledged to be symbols of mediated power.

> In this manner, Zionist dress, like the bricolages of such protest movements as cargo cults, appropriates select signs of colonial dominance, turning historical symbols of oppression into dynamic forces of transcendence. With the same logic, the satin banners incorporate military pomp, evoking the aggressive Protestant image of "soldiers of the Lord"; the letter H affixed to them suggests perhaps a double cross, but is also emblematic of the power of literacy itself . . . . For literacy has been a crucial marker of the forces that subjugate the uneducated peasant (Comaroff 1985: 225–6).

Comaroff's research sheds light on the case of the women religious and their different but related set of issues. The Tshidi used symbols of resistance, i.e. dress, related to both colonialism and the missionaries in mediating their identity. In a similar manner, the women religious in this study also used dress in their politics of resistance to emerge from their socialization into the order prior to Vatican II to the liminality surrounding Vatican II, and finally in the mediation of their social and personal identities. In both studies, the spirit of resistance was one that facilitated the reality of existing within the respective social systems. Like the Tshidi who adapted to colonialism and the missionaries, women religious in this study during a period of demanded social change chose to remain within their orders rather than abandon them. For both the Tshidi and the women religious, their new identities symbolically reflected and constructed by their dress demonstrated their ability to protest and yet remain within the system. Their ability to appropriate fashions of the secular world indicated their ability to mediate between the demands of a consumer society and their vow of poverty.

This study of women religious provides a model for examining how changes in enduring modes of dress such as habits can be examined not only in relation to the more predominantly held view of changing social roles but also from the perspective of personal identity. There are broader cross-cultural implications to this study. For example, the current movement in Egypt among lower-middle-class women to return to veiling practices is viewed as a regressive stance in relation to social roles by many Westerners and non-Muslims. MacLeod (1991) conveys in her research a culturally and ideologically complex motivation for this return to veiling, highly rooted in issues of agency, identity and personal ideology. Rapid social change in Egypt has created cultural discontinuity, causing these largely urban women to "turn back to a more authentic and culturally true way of life, and they perceive the veil as part of this cultural reformation" (MacLeod 1991: 111). Westerners quickly view the return to veiling as a regressive step in relation to women's expanding social roles within that society; but have they considered more personal issues of identity and social mediation? MacLeod's research, ethnographic and interview-based, allows us to have deeper insight. The relationship between dress and social change must be carefully examined, as with women religious, by examining their relationship to social role and issues of social and personal identity and the mediation of these through the symbol of dress.

Davis (1992: 26) uses the term *fault lines* to describe "culturally induced strains concerning who and what we are" that find expression in dress. Vatican II certainly unleashed a seismic shock for women religious; but the forces of change within orders ultimately came from the women themselves in the form of human agency. Women religious were poised and ready to address issues of role, identity and social change.

Notes

1. Some women in the study used this word to elaborate on how they felt wearing a habit. This is not my choice of words. The term *androgyny* is derived from the Greek words *aner* (man) and *gyne* (woman). Heilbrun (1964) uses this term to define a condition in which the characteristics of the sexes and the human impulses expressed by men and women are not rigidly assigned. Therefore, the term may be more closely associated with perceptions of identity than solely of characteristics associated with physical appearance.
2. In one interview, a woman spoke of her awareness that some women used subtle deviances in the way they wore their habits to express "vanity," "style," and "worldliness." Personal agency among women who wore and do wear habits will bear future research. Boynton-Arthur (1993a) examined agency in women's dress among the patriarchal structure and strict appearance codes of Mennonite society.
3. Ebaugh's (1993: ix) current research documents the fact that women's religious orders are "a dying institution in this country."

References

Baer, D. and Mosele, V. 1970. "Political and religious beliefs of Catholics and attitudes toward lay dress of Sisters." *The Journal of Psychology*, 74: 77–83.

Bourdieu, P. 1977. *Outline of a Theory of Practice*, trans. R. Nice. Cambridge: Cambridge University Press.

Boynton-Arthur, L. 1993a. Clothing, control, and women's agency: The mitigation of patriarchal power. In S. Fisher and K. Davis (eds), *Negotiating at the Margins: The Gendered Discourses of Power and Resistance*, pp. 66–84. Rutgers, NJ: Rutgers University Press.

——. 1993b. "The applicability of ethnography and grounded theory to clothing and textile research." In S. Lennon and L. Burns (eds), *ITAA special publication #5*, pp. 137–45. Monument, CO: ITAA.

Bush, G. and London, P. 1960. "On the disappearance of knickers," *Journal of Social Psychology*, 43: 359–66.

Carlan, M. 1979. "Who cares how nuns dress?" *The Catholic Digest*, March: 100–4.

Ceremonial for the Reception of Novices for the Sisters of Providence. 1913. Springfield: Diocese of Springfield Massachusetts.

Comaroff, J. 1985. *Body of Power, Spirit of Resistance*. Chicago, IL: University of Chicago Press.

Davis, F. 1992. *Fashion, Culture and Identity*. Chicago, IL: University of Chicago Press.

Decree for Renewal of Religious Life. 1962. NCWC translation, Number 17.

Douglas, M. 1966. *Purity and Danger: An Analysis of Concepts of Pollution and Taboo*. Washington: Frederick Praeger.

——. 1970. *Natural Symbols*. New York: Vintage Books.

Durkheim, E. and Mauss, M. (1963). *Primitive Classification*, trans. R. Needham. London: Cohen & West.

Ebaugh, H. 1977. *Out of the Cloister: A Study of Organizational Dilemmas*. Austin: University of Texas Press.

——. 1993. *Women in the Vanishing Cloister*. New Brunswick, NJ: Rutgers University Press.

Elizabeth, M. 1965. "Modernizing the religious habit – II." *Sponsa Regis*, Vol. 36: 279–82.

Glaser, B. and Strauss, A. 1967. *The Discovery of Grounded Theory*. Chicago: Aldine Publishing Co.

Goffman, E. 1959. *The Presentation of Self in Everyday Life*. New York: Doubleday.

——. 1963. *Stigma: Notes on the Management of a Spoiled Identity*. Englewood Cliffs, NJ: Prentice Hall.

Griffin, M. 1975. *Unbelling the Cat. The Courage to Choose*. Boston: Little Brown.

Heilbrun, C. 1964. *Toward a Recognition of Androgyny*. New York: Alfred A. Knopf, Inc.

Hoelter, J. (1985). "A structural theory of personal consistency." *Social Psychology Quarterly*, 48 (2): 118–29.

Joseph, N. and Alex, N. 1972. "The uniform: A sociological perspective." *American Journal of Sociology*, 77: 719–30.

Kaiser, S. 1990. *The Social Psychology of Clothing*. (2nd ed.) New York: Macmillan.

Kaiser, S., Nagasawa, R. and Hutton, S. 1995. "Construction of an SI theory of fashion: Part 1, ambivalence and change." *Clothing and Textiles Research Journal*, 13, (3): 172–83.

Lesousky, A. 1967. "The religious habit: A new approach." *Sisters Today*, Vol. 38: 312–14.

Lifton, J. 1961. *Thought Reform and the Psychology of Totalism*. New York: Norton.

Marx, K. 1967. *Capital: A Critique of Political Economy*, 3 vols. New York: International Publishers.

Mauss, M. 1973. "Techniques of the body," trans. B. Brewster. *Economy and Society*, 2 (1): 70–88.

Metz, J. 1968. *Poverty of Spirit*. NY: Paulist Press.

Michelman, S. 1992. Dress in Kalabari women's societies. Unpublished doctoral dissertation. University of Minnesota, St. Paul.

Michelman, S., and Eicher, J. 1995. "Dress and gender in Kalabari women's societies." *Clothing and Textiles Research Journal*, 13(2): 121–130.

Michelman, S. 1995. "Social change and the symbolism of dress in Kalabari women's societies." *Family and Consumer Sciences Research Journal*, Vol. 23, No. 4: 368–392.

Nagasawa, R., Kaiser, S. and Hutton, S. 1996. "Construction of an SI theory of fashion: Part 3. Context of explanation." *Clothing and Textiles Research Journal*, 14, (1): 54–62.

Neussendorfer, M. 1964. "Modernizing the religious habit." *Sponsa Regis*, Vol. 36 (3): 67–79.

Obeyesekere, G. 1981. *Medusa's Hair*. Chicago, IL.: University of Chicago Press.

Plogsterth, A. 1975. "The Modernization of Roman Catholic Sisters' Habits in the United States in the 1950's and 1960's." *Dress*, (1): 7–15.

Reinharz, S. 1992. *Feminist Methods in Social Research*. Oxford: Oxford University Press.

Roach-Higgins, M. and Eicher, J. 1993. "Dress and identity." *ITAA special publication #5*.

Roberts, W. 1967. "The religious habit and contemporary witness." *Sisters Today*, Vol. 38: 267–75.

SanGiovanni, L. 1978. *Ex-nuns*. Norwood, NJ: Ablex Publishing.

Snow, D. and Anderson, L. (1987). "Identity work among the homeless: The verbal construction and avowal of personal identities." *American Journal of Sociology*, Vol. 92 (6): 1336–71.

Stone, G. 1962. "Appearance and the self." In A. Rose (ed.), *Human Behavior and Social Processes: An Interactionist Approach*, pp. 86–118. New York: Houghton, Mifflin Co.

Strauss, A. 1987. *Qualitative Analysis for Social Scientists*. Cambridge: Cambridge University Press.

Tate, J. 1967. "Religious habits and psychology of dress." *Sisters Today*, Vol. 38: 276–9.

Turner, R. 1968. "Sociological aspects of role." In D. Sills (ed.), *International Encyclopedia of the Social Sciences*, Vol. 13 pp. 552–6. New York: Macmillan and Free Press.

Turner, V. 1967. *The Forest of Symbols*. Ithaca: Cornell University Press.

Van Gennep, A. 1960. *The Rites of Passage*, trans. M. B. Vizedom and G. L. Caffee. Chicago: University of Chicago Press.

Fashion Theory, Volume 2, Issue 2, pp.193–196
Reprints available directly from the Publishers.
Photocopying permitted by licence only.

Reviewed by
Jonathan Schroeder

Book Review

Twilight Zones: The Hidden Life of Cultural Images from Plato to O. J. **by Susan Bordo, University of California Press, 1997**

278 pp., illustrated, bibliographic notes, index

Despite its rather clunky title, *Twilight Zones: The Hidden Life of Cultural Images from Plato to O. J.* marks the emergence of a major cultural theorist and commentator. Susan Bordo's new book concerns itself with images from fashion, film, television, and advertising. Bordo, a rare philosopher who deals with issues of fashion, describes her work this way: "I have always considered myself a phenomenologist and diagnostician of culture who uses diverse theoretical tools to excavate and expose hidden or unquestioned aspects of concrete forms, occurrences, texts, practices" (p. 174). She takes images seriously, and is concerned with their power to influence: "For us, bedazzlement by created images is no metaphor; it is the actual condition of our lives . . . The technology for producing them is far more sophisticated, and those who produce the images seem to have no compunction about using that technology in the service of a deceptive verisimilitude" (p. 2).

In *Twilight Zones*, Bordo takes up concerns from her successful 1993 book *Unbearable Weight: Feminism, Western Culture, and the Body*, which introduced a philosophical analysis of the connections between media images, eating disorders, and controlling metaphors of the body. She writes from her role as both consumer and critic, and interweaves personal narrative with rigorous analysis of images and discourse. In chapters such as "Braveheart, Babe, and the Contemporary Body" she holds forth on topics such as gender, cosmetic surgery, and ethnicity in films, advertising, and television. She especially focuses on recent writings that view cosmetic surgery as liberating for women by carefully sifting through arguments about appearance, agency, and the body. She describes her own thoughts about cosmetic dentistry, after a friendly dentist recommended $25,000 worth of cosmetic work to improve her smile (she declined).

Her willingness to discuss her feelings, thoughts, temptations, and responses to images is a powerful technique that brings her points home. She eschews an objective standpoint, but finds interpretation, too, a messy thing: "In a world in which appearances can be so skillfully manipulated, the notion that everything is 'open to interpretation' is no longer an entirely edifying one. Without toppling into absolutist conceptions of truth, we need to rehabilitate the notion that not all versions of reality are equally trustworthy, equally deserving of our assent" (p. 12). What Bordo provides is a framework for thinking critically about images and their influence. She is careful to ground her analysis in social, cultural, and philosophical history, and she insists on the influential roles images play in society. At the same time, she is not above image worship—she confesses her fascination with cultural images in a way that makes her analysis more forceful. Bordo writes not with a condescending, above-it-all attitude, but rather with an engaged, thoroughly immersed critical eye.

Advertising represents a basic paradox of a consumer society—hundreds of thousands of people buy the same products and feel they are bold and individual for doing so. Consumers are instructed to take charge of their lives and bodies through consumption—we now are told that we are producing something through consumption. I call this phenomenon *hyperaffluence*, a state in which consumption is no longer about meeting physical needs, but rather psychological longings.

Dissatisfaction, Bordo argues, is the "essence of advertising and the fuel of consumer capitalism, which cannot allow equilibrium or stasis in human desire. Thus, we are not permitted to feel satisfied with ourselves and we are 'empowered' only and always through fantasies of what we *could* be" (p. 51). She discusses the role doctors and clinics play in promoting cosmetic surgery by creating defects and undermining confidence in one's appearance. She devastates arguments that cosmetic surgery empowers people: "for cosmetic surgery is more than an individual choice; it is a burgeoning industry and an increasingly normative cultural practice. As such, it is a significant contributory *cause* of women's suffering by continually upping the ante on what counts as an acceptable face and body" (p. 43). She discusses criticisms of her work that accuse her of being an essentialist, that is, ignoring how the body is constructed, and responds by pointing out the lived experience of women's bodies: "My work on the body is more 'material' than that of many of philosophers because I believe that the study of representations and cultural 'discourse,' while an important part of the cultural study of the body, cannot by itself stand as a history of the body. Those discourses impinge on us as fleshy bodies, often in ways that cannot be determined from a study of representations alone" (p. 183).

She turns her eye toward racial issues in an analysis of several recent media cases, including the Anita Hill/Clarence Thomas affair, the Bob Packwood diaries, and, of course, the O. J. Simpson trial. Her analysis of the O. J. trial provides a useful example of her analytical approach, in which she aims to "encourage historical perspective, nonreductionist understanding, clear and rigorous thinking, skepticism about sound bites and slick images, the exercise of informed and reasoned judgment" (p. 105). In discussing the O. J. case, she makes provocative links between the televised trial, contemporary advertising, and the image of Black Africa, which has been constructed as savage, primitive. She reproduces the notorious Guess jeans ad, which presented an O. J. look-alike behind a blond female model—a not so subtle reference to the racial, gender, and cultural images associated with the trial. Her insights into the O. J. trial are fascinating and edifying, and one wishes for more, as sometimes she jumps from incident to incident.

In her chapter "Never Just Pictures" she moves into the central premise of the book, the relationships between images, culture, and social history. She hammers away at criticisms of her concern for images by discussing how images work in consumer culture: "Today, teenagers no longer have the luxury of a distinction between what's required of a fashion model and what's required of them; the perfected images have become our dominant reality and have set standards for us all—standards that are increasingly *un*real in their demands on us" (p. 116). She is careful not to misplace concern about images with lived experience, and emphasizes that she is interested in what images express. She takes up the issue of objectification, and injects a useful way of thinking about how objectification operates: "Once we recognize that we never respond only to particular body parts or their configuration but always to the meanings they carry for us, the old feminist charge of 'objectification' seems inadequate to describe what is going on when women's bodies are depicted in sexualized or aestheticized ways. The notion of women-as-objects suggests the reduction of women to 'mere' bodies, when actually what's going on is often far more disturbing than that, involving the depiction of regressive ideals of feminine behavior and attitude that go much deeper than appearance" (p. 124). Thus, she opens up possibilities of discussing images as more than just representations of particular people, or particular bodies. A major contribution of *Twilight Zones* is to provide a framework for understanding what Bordo calls the hidden life of cultural images, through a method grounded in phenomenology, cultural analysis, and perhaps most critically, taking images seriously as societal forces.

Fashion Theory, Volume 2, Issue 2, pp.197–200
Reprints available directly from the Publishers.
Photocopying permitted by licence only.

Reviewed by
S. K. Hopkins

Book Review

British Military Spectacle – From the Napoleonic Wars through the Crimea **by Scott Hughes Myerly, Harvard University Press, 1996**

293 pp., illustrated, bibliography, index

The title of *British Military Spectacle* gives little away, and it is by consulting the dust jacket flaps that one is informed that Scott Hughes Myerly's book is about British Army Uniforms, which "played a powerful role in the troops' performance on campaign, in battle, and as dramatic entertainment in peacetime." It is perhaps fortunate that the dust jacket provides this information, as it is not until p. 11 that the author, himself, gives details of the book's intention which is to show how "this imagery ['manipulation of visual images' by the State] was an essential component of military management in the British Army . . . the martial spectacles were essential in communicating to soldiers the fundamental values embedded in the military model: bravery and duty, discipline, self-control, conformity, order, and hierarchy; unity and solidarity of purpose; motivation, efficiency and self sacrifice for a higher goal; and above all, loyalty to those in command."

Thus Myerly himself does not regard his work as a book on uniform. However, there is barely a page which doesn't mention the wearing apparel of the British soldier, and it is certainly refreshing that an attempt has been made to provide information on British Army Uniform other than "who-wore-what-when-and-where" books. In many ways Myerly has achieved his goals; his hypotheses are good and there are certainly openings for further research into the points he makes. The chapter on Entertainment, Power and Paradigm is well thought out and should prove inspirational to any student of British Military Uniform to move into different areas of research other than the aforementioned route of the five Ws.

Myerly's bibliography and notes take up over a third of the 293 pages of text, yet not one book on British Military Uniform is mentioned. The author endeavors to cover the lack of such volumes in the bibliography on p. 9: "Although there are many antiquarian and collector books about military dress, a number of which are supported by excellent research, only rarely has the subject been deemed worthy of scholarly analysis." In the notes on p. 202 (note 49) four books only are quoted. All these works are good and worthy of their genre; but apart from more detailed contemporary illustrations they all follow, very closely, the excellent lead of the two pioneers of the history of British Military Uniforms, the late Major C. C. P. Lawson and Mr W. Y. Carman, still happily in the present. Sadly, Myerly has been too dismissive of the books available on British Military Uniform. He might have been well advised to have studied *The Dress of the Royal Artillery* by D. Alastair Campbell (Arms and Armour Press, London, 1971), an excellent, well-researched book that this reviewer constantly recommends, together with (despite its lack of relevance to Myerly's present volume), *British Army Uniforms and Insignia of World War Two* by Brian L. Davis (Arms and Armour Press) as model works on uniform. As any costume historian knows, no period can be dealt with in isolation; and it is surprising that no mention is made of that stalwart work that no one attempting to write on late eighteenth-century or early nineteenth-century uniform should be without, *British Military Uniforms 1768–1796* by Hugh Strachan (Arms and Armour Press, London, 1975). Nowhere are mentioned *Officers' Dress Regulations* or the three books based on Dress Regulations covering Waterloo and the Crimean War by the Mollo Brothers and Michael Barthorpe.

It is probably because of Mr. Myerly's dismissive attitude to books on uniform by authors of works other than those specifically mentioned by him that errors and statements that could be misleading on the matter of British Military Dress have occurred. We are told on p. 19 that "Facing colours" [sic] often varied over the years with the changing taste of the colonel and the officers. "Often" is somewhat open-ended and misleading. Between 1768 and 1881 one regiment of Heavy Cavalry altered the facing colour. Of the 100 Line Infantry Regiments originally raised on the British Establishment, only 15 changed the facing colour between 1768 and 1881. Of those, one regiment became Rifles and adopted a completely different style of uniform and 10 became Royal, which automatically made them eligible for blue facings. Only 4 Infantry regiments therefore altered their facing colour without change of role in 113 years. Of these, only one altered the colour twice. Indeed, of the 100 Regiments on the establishment in 1881 only two had had more than one change of facing from the time of their raising. Myerly's statement could only be regarded as marginally correct regarding the Light Dragoons. Dye batches, wear and tear frequently altered the *shade* of the facing colour; but not the colour. On the same page we are informed that white lace was worn by other ranks. Two sentences later we are informed that the lace had worms and that the loops were bastion or rectangular in shape. We are not told that white lace was worn by Sergeants until *c.* 1836, when the worms were discontinued for other ranks' lace. There also is an omission among the loop shapes which is that of the pointed loop. Page 59 states that recruiters sometimes wore officers' clothing. No date is given, and the note provides no source for this statement. Such statements as "The Cavalry wore blue for the most part (except during William IV's reign)" are, again, misleading. With the exception of the Royal Horse Guards, all Heavy Cavalry wore scarlet. Only the 6th Dragoon Guards wore a blue uniform, and that from 1853. The Light Cavalry, however, were predominantly dressed in blue during the period covered by the book.

There is a general vagueness in the text regarding dates. One example is on p. 91, where the use of white feathers for Grenadier Companies and green for Light Infantry is mentioned. But other ranks did not wear feather plumes in the Infantry: they wore worsted plumes or tufts. In 1835 the feather plume of the officers and the plume-tuft of the other ranks were replaced by the ball-tuft, of which the only mention is in the plate captions where it is referred to as a "pom-pom."

Another example is the penultimate and last paragraphs on p. 43, discussing the designing of uniforms, which have no dates except in the notes. However, the only dates provided in the notes are those of the publication of the source, with a possible date-range of 1796 to 1846.

Although this is probably not the fault of the author, because of the constant necessity to consult the notes it is irritating that they are housed at the rear of the book. Many could well have been incorporated into the text.

Although one has to accept the American spelling of certain words, to Americanize the title of a famous Regiment such as the Royal Scots Greys seems somewhat impolite. The lack of the use of capital letters does tend to be confusing. We learn on p. 112 that the artillery wore blue coats, which would seem to indicate that the guns were dressed in some form of coat, rather than that the Royal Artillery, or Artillery units, wore a blue garment.

It would have been helpful for the author to have consulted works on British military flags. Not all flags were painted; many were embroidered. Not all Cavalry flags were Standards; the Light Cavalry carried Guidons.

Moving on from the subjects of uniform and vexillology, the author does not appear to understand the structure of the British Army. On p. 23, the Yeomanry Cavalry is referred to as Militia Cavalry, and on p. 63 the Fencibles (Cavalry or Infantry?) are also referred to as Militia. The Yeomanry, Fencibles and Militia were all entirely different forces within the British Army. I note that there is no mention in the bibliography of the Hon. J. W. Fortescue's *A History of the British Army* (London, 1906) and C. Sebag-Montefiore's *A History of the Volunteer Forces* (London, 1908), both classic works that explain such details.

Finally, one sincerely hopes that no member of the Royal Company of Archers reads p. 146. For the Queen's Body Guard for Scotland to be reduced to a sporting club might just cause an uprising in the Highlands and Lowlands.

In conclusion, the idea behind the book is excellent. It is just so very sad that the author did not spend more time on reading those rapidly dismissed books on uniform or the basic books on the British Army, in addition to carefully observing the fabric, cut and style of extant uniforms. With so many misleading remarks, one has one's doubts about the validity of the remainder of the text. The study of the British Army and its uniforms is highly complex, and not to be taken lightly. What a wonderful book this might have been in the hands of a true expert such as W. Y. Carman!

Fashion Theory, Volume 2, Issue 2, pp.201–204
Reprints available directly from the Publishers.
Photocopying permitted by licence only.

Dress on Display Conference, Victoria & Albert Museum, 17–18 July 1998

A two-day conference looking at issues around the nature of exhibiting clothing—including conservation, mannequin display and design and how the method in which dress is displayed affects its interpretation—will be held in the Lecture Theatre of the Victoria & Albert Museum on Friday and Saturday, the 17–18 of July 1998. The conference has been jointly organized by the Courtauld History of Dress Association (CHODA) and the V&A. Full rate is £28 per day. Concessions are available. For further details and to book please contact the V&A Box Office on +44(0)171-938-8407.

Fashion and Dress in Asia Conference, Hong Kong, Spring, 1999

ConsumAsiaN (consumption in Asia) research network is planning to hold a conference on fashion and dress in Asia in the spring of 1999. The conference will cover the persistence and transformation of clothes traditions along with the most recent developments in trend and youth fashion. It will address the way in which dress can articulate key cultural issues such as the interface between tradition and modernization, ethnic/national self-definition and imperialism, East and West, and the global and the local. Further it will relate to other markers of identity, such as gender, age, class, etc.

For more information please contact:
ConsumAsiaN
Department of Japanese Studies
University of Hong Kong
Pokfulam Road
Hong Kong
Fax: +852-2548-7399
e-mail: consumas@hku.hk

Fashion Theory, Volume 2, Issue 2, pp.205–206
Reprints available directly from the Publishers.

Call for Manuscripts

Papers are being solicited for a book on dress, culture and religion. Qualitative/ethnographic research on groups outside of the US is needed which will examine the social control of the body through religio-cultural dress norms. Please send an abstract to LARTHUR@HAWAII.EDU.

Notes for Contributors

Articles should be approximately 25 pages in length and *must* include a three-sentence biography of the author(s). Interviews should not exceed 15 pages and do not require an author biography. Film, exhibition and book reviews are normally 500 to 1,000 words in length. The Publishers will require a disk as well as a hard copy of any contributions (please mark clearly on the disk what word-processing program has been used).

Fashion Theory: The Journal of Dress, Body & Culture will produce one issue a year devoted to a single topic. Persons wishing to organize a topical issue are invited to submit a proposal which contains a hundred-word description of the topic together with a list of potential contributors and paper subjects. Proposals are accepted only after review by the journal editor and in-house editorial staff at Berg Publishers.

Manuscripts
Manuscripts should be submitted to: *Fashion Theory: The Journal of Dress, Body & Culture*. Manuscripts will be acknowledged by the editor and entered into the review process discussed below. Manuscripts without illustrations will not be returned unless the author provides a self-addressed stamped envelope. Submission of a manuscript to the journal will be taken to imply that it is not being considered elsewhere for publication, and that if accepted for publication, it will not be published elsewhere, in the same form, in any language, without the consent of the editor and publisher. It is a condition of acceptance by the editor of a manuscript for publication that the publishers automatically acquire the copyright of the published article throughout the world. *Fashion Theory: The Journal of Dress, Body & Culture* does not pay authors for their manuscripts nor does it provide retyping, drawing, or mounting of illustrations.

Style
U.S. spelling and mechanicals are to be used. Authors are advised to consult *The Chicago Manual of Style (14th Edition)* as a guideline for style. *Webster's Dictionary* is our arbiter of spelling. We encourage the use of major subheadings and, where appropriate, second-level subheadings. Manuscripts submitted for consideration as an article must contain: a title page with the full title of the article, the author(s) name and address, and a three-sentence biography for each author. Do not place the author's name on any other page of the manuscript.

Manuscript Preparation
Manuscripts must be typed double-spaced (including quotations, notes, and references cited), one side only, with at least one-inch margins on standard paper using a typeface no smaller than 12pts. The original manuscript and a copy of the text on disk *(please ensure it is clearly marked with the word-processing program that has been used) must* be submitted, along with black and white *original* photographs (to be returned). Authors should retain a copy for their records. Any necessary artwork *must* be submitted with the manuscript.

Footnotes

Footnotes appear as 'Notes' at the end of articles. Authors are advised to include footnote material in the text whenever possible. Notes are to be numbered consecutively throughout the paper and are to be typed double-spaced at the end of the text. (Do not use any footnoting or end-noting programs which your software may offer as this text becomes irretrievably lost at the typesetting stage.)

References

The list of references should be limited to, and inclusive of, those publications actually cited in the text. References are to be cited in the body of the text in parentheses with author's last name, the year of original publication, and page number—e.g., (Rouch 1958: 45). Titles and publication information appear as 'References' at the end of the article and should be listed alphabetically by author and chronologically for each author. Names of journals and publications should appear in full. Film and video information appears as 'Filmography'. References cited should be typed double-spaced on a separate page. *References not presented in the style required will be returned to the author for revision.*

Tables

All tabular material should be part of a separately numbered series of 'Tables'. Each table must be typed on a separate sheet and identified by a short descriptive title. Footnotes for tables appear at the bottom of the table. Marginal notations on manuscripts should indicate approximately where tables are to appear.

Figures

All illustrative material (drawings, maps, diagrams, and photographs) should be designated 'Figures'. They must be submitted in a form suitable for publication without redrawing. Drawings should be carefully done with black ink on either hard, white, smooth-surfaced board or good quality tracing paper. Ordinarily, computer-generated drawings are not of publishable quality. Photographs should be black and white glossy prints (the publishers will not accept color) and should be numbered on the back to key with captions. Whenever possible, photographs should be 8 x 10 inches. All figures should be numbered consecutively. All captions should be typed double-spaced on a separate page. Marginal notations on manuscripts should indicate approximately where figures are to appear. While the editors and publishers will use ordinary care in protecting all figures submitted, they cannot assume responsibility for their loss or damage. Authors are discouraged from submitting rare or non-replaceable materials. It is the author's responsibility to secure written copyright clearance on *all* photographs and drawings that are not in the public domain.

Criteria for Evaluation

Fashion Theory: The Journal of Dress, Body & Culture is a refereed journal. Manuscripts will be accepted only after review by both the editors and anonymous reviewers deemed competent to make professional judgments concerning the quality of the manuscript. Upon request, authors will receive reviewers' evaluations.

Reprints for Authors

Twenty-five reprints of authors' articles will be provided to the first named author free of charge. Additional reprints may be purchased upon request.